Lectures on Musical Life

William Sterndale Bennett

British Music 1600–1900

ISSN 1752–1904

Series Editors

RACHEL COWGILL and PETER HOLMAN
(Leeds University, Centre for English Music)

This series provides a forum for the best new work in this area; it takes a deliberately inclusive approach, covering immigrants and emigrants as well as native musicians. Contributions on all aspects of seventeenth-, eighteenth- and nineteenth-century British music studies are welcomed, particularly those placing music in its social and historical contexts, and addressing Britain's musical links with Europe and the rest of the globe.

Proposals or queries should be sent in the first instance to Dr Rachel Cowgill, Dr Peter Holman or Boydell & Brewer at the addresses shown below. All submissions will receive prompt and informed consideration.

Dr Rachel Cowgill, School of Music, University of Leeds, Leeds, LS2 9JT
email: r.e.cowgill@leeds.ac.uk

Dr Peter Holman, School of Music, University of Leeds, Leeds, LS2 9JT
email: p.k.holman@leeds.ac.uk

Boydell & Brewer Ltd, PO Box 9, Woodbridge, Suffolk, IP12 3DF
email: editorial@boydell.co.uk

William Sterndale Bennett, aged about 50

Lectures on Musical Life

William Sterndale Bennett

Edited with an introduction by
Nicholas Temperley
with the assistance of Yunchung Yang

THE BOYDELL PRESS

First published 2006
The Boydell Press, Woodbridge

ISBN 1 84383 272 0

The Boydell Press is an imprint of Boydell & Brewer Ltd
PO Box 9, Woodbridge, Suffolk IP12 3DF, UK
and of Boydell & Brewer Inc.,
668 Mt Hope Avenue, Rochester, NY 14620, USA
website: www.boydellandbrewer.com

A CIP catalogue record for this book is available from the British Library

This publication is printed on acid-free paper

Typeset by Pru Harrison, Hacheston, Suffolk
Printed in Great Britain by
MPG Books Ltd, Cornwall

Contents

List of Plates

Foreword

This edition is the outcome of my lifelong interest in William Sterndale Bennett, which has been generously supported by the composer's family. His grandson, Robert Sterndale-Bennett (1880–1963), who was for many years director of music at Uppingham School, offered help, advice, and hospitality in the early years of my research, and the tradition has been maintained by Robert's grandson, Barry Sterndale-Bennett. The lectures are published here by Barry's permission. I am most grateful for this, and also for his continued assistance and support at every stage of the work.

I would like to express my thanks to Yunchung Yang, who earned a DMA degree from the University of Illinois for her research on Sterndale Bennett's Fantasia for piano. Dr Yang made the initial transcription of the lectures on which this edition is based, and has undertaken numerous investigations to assist in the annotation of the lectures and in the writing of the Introduction.

I am indebted to the University of Illinois for financial support and photographic assistance, and to Cambridge University Library for allowing me to consult the university archives. I am also grateful to Katherine Syer for advice on Wagnerian matters, and to Elisabeth Agate, Christina Bashford, Paul Collen, Alison Latham, Philip Oswald, and Anne Stow for their assistance in locating illustrations.

I must also express my thanks to the following for permission to reproduce visual materials: Barry Sterndale-Bennett (Frontispiece and Plates 4 and 9); Country Life Picture Library (Plate 1); Sheffield Local Studies Library (Plate 2); Her Majesty's Stationery Office (Plate 3); Bärenreiter Verlag (Plate 7); and the University of Illinois (Plates 5, 6, and 8).

N. T.
Urbana, Illinois
April 2006

Textual Note

The sole source for the text of these lectures is a set of six bound notebooks in Mr Barry Sterndale-Bennett's possession at Longparish, Andover, Hampshire. They form part of the composer's library, which has been kept substantially intact by the family for four generations. They contain both drafts and fair copies of lectures in Bennett's hand; certain portions in the hand of his wife Mary; a few odd notes that may have had a bearing on the lectures; and some printed syllabuses and programmes pertaining to them.

The fair copies have been used as copy-texts for the twelve selected lectures. The drafts have been examined; in the few cases where they contain significant passages later omitted or altered in the fair copies, they are quoted in footnotes. Printed programmes of performed musical examples used to illustrate Lectures 1–8 have been consulted, and where they differ from written designations of the examples found in the text, this fact has been mentioned in a footnote.

I have silently corrected and modernised capitalisation, spelling, and punctuation, except where there is ambiguity, in which case an explanatory footnote is provided. Bennett often used a dash (–) or even occasionally a double dash (=) in cases where other or no punctuation would be used today (see Plate 4, p. 19). His own usage in citing titles of works has been retained. Underlines have been reproduced, except in cases where they denote the beginning of a new idea and appear to be intended to guide the lecturer in his oral delivery of the lectures.

Editorial additions are shown in square brackets [ ]. Where Bennett has misstated a name, date, or historical fact, or used an obsolete expression, a correction or gloss has generally been supplied by means of brackets or a footnote. But where his broader summations do not agree with prevailing modern views derived from subsequent research or altered historical judgements, they have generally been left intact without comment.

Passages deleted in the source are ignored if the deletion can be attributed to correction of an error, avoidance of repetition, or improved euphony. If the deletion or substitution shows an apparent change of mind on a significant point, the deleted word or phrase is printed in angle brackets < >.

Similarly, passages added in the source to an already completed text are printed without special designation if they represent the correction of an accidental omission or the clarification of meaning. If the addition is significant in itself, or if it replaces a deleted passage shown in angle brackets, it is printed in curly brackets { }.

A special situation relates to the repetition of Lectures 1 and 2 at Sheffield. Some of the corrections made by Bennett in the text clearly relate to the Sheffield presentation in one of three ways: to give due recognition to local or regional phenomena such as the Bradford and Leeds Festivals; to revise statements that pertained specifically to conditions in London; or to allude to the particular musical examples that were to be performed at Sheffield. Here the London reading is given in the main text and the Sheffield revision in a footnote. In many other cases, there is no way of knowing whether a given correction was made for London or for Sheffield, and it has been treated in the normal way.

Specimens of music that were performed at the London Institution in the course of Lectures 1–8 have been listed in rectangular frames at the points where they occurred in the lectures. The musical programmes for the two Sheffield lectures are given in the Appendix, along with the programme notes with which Bennett introduced the first set.

An effort has been made to trace the sources of verbal quotations. Literary sources cited by Bennett are left without editorial amplification in the text, but are fully identified in the Bibliography, as are works referred to by short citations in the footnotes and index. Musical works that are not completely described have been identified, if possible, and the additional information has been placed in square brackets or footnotes. (All footnotes are editorial.) In quotations from primary sources other than the lectures themselves, three dots are used to represent omitted passages.

Persons, institutions and organisations mentioned, if not generally familiar, are identified in the Index.

Introduction

In the current revival of interest in British musical life of the 19th century, much new research has been done on the economic history of music and musical institutions. The writings of the economic historian Cyril Ehrlich,[1] and of many who have been influenced by him, have shown how far the composition, performance, and reception of music were governed by material self-interest.[2] There is no question that this body of work has brought a new realism and balance to the study of the period. As one reviewer put it, 'the British musical scene in this period was one driven by the commercial impetus to a far greater extent than that of any other country'.[3]

There is another side of the matter that requires equal attention: the influence of intellectual, spiritual, and aesthetic leadership on the taste of consumers of music, regardless of economic or social factors. One important channel by which knowledge and taste in music were disseminated was the public lecture, which gained a new prominence in 19th-century Britain.

Public Lectures on Music

Public lecturing in England on secular topics can be traced to Sir Thomas Gresham (1518–79), who made provision in his will for 'a college in London for the gratuitous instruction of all who choose to attend the lectures'. Lectureships were endowed in seven subjects: divinity, rhetoric, geometry, medical science, astronomy, law, and music. John Bull, the first Gresham professor of music, began lecturing in 1596. But in the following centuries the Gresham lectures fell into neglect. Significant lectures on music were given only on isolated occasions during the 18th

1 In particular, *The Music Profession in Britain* and *First Philharmonic*.

2 A key volume is Bashford and Langley, *Music and British Culture 1785–1914*. According to its jacket it 'embraces the music marketplace, piano culture, musicians' work patterns, music institutions and audiences, concert and repertoire history, issues in performance, criticism and reception, gender, and national and urban identities.'

3 Paul Rodmell, review of Bashford and Langley, *Music and British Culture 1785–1914*, in *Nineteenth-Century Music Review*, 1/1 (2004), 156.

century, and most approached the subject from a scientific or philosophical standpoint.[1]

A new era of public lecturing began in 1800 when the Royal Institution, founded by the American-born Count Rumford, began to promote lectures at its premises in Albemarle Street, London, for improving knowledge of science and encouraging practical inventions. In 1805 music was added to the list of subjects covered, and regular courses of lectures on music date from that year. Several other organisations followed suit during the next few decades, in London, Edinburgh, and other cities across the country.

William Crotch, who was the first lecturer on music at the Royal Institution, was also professor of music at Oxford, and had already, on his own initiative, established the first lectures in music at either university, beginning in 1798.[2] His purpose was not to advance the science of music but, in his own words, 'an endeavour to raise the taste'.[3] An important innovation was the use of live illustrations played by Crotch himself at the piano, assisted by an orchestra; this ensured that the subject matter, however abstruse, would be plainly linked to music as a concrete experience. Since Oxford had no music students as such, Crotch's audience was presumably a general group of local music lovers and performers. His subject matter was the history of music from ancient times until the present. He depended to a great extent on Charles Burney's *General History of Music* (1776–89), and he also adapted some theories of art and taste from Joshua Reynolds's *Discourses on Painting* (1769–91).[4]

Crotch continually revised and repeated his lectures over the next three decades, and from 1805 they were frequently offered at the Royal Institution. Eventually, in 1831, he published them in their final form.[5] The musical examples, however, had appeared much earlier, in 1807, as *Specimens of Various Styles of Music*. They were a valuable anthology of music of all kinds, including 'national' (folk) music and non-Western music, fields in which Crotch was something of a pioneer. As Vincent Duckles points out, Crotch in his musical studies belonged to the 'aesthetic' school of thought, descended from North and Burney, rather than the 'scientific', deriving from Pepusch and Hawkins.[6] Both lines

[1] They are well documented in Kassler, *Science of Music,* and in Kassler, 'Royal Institution Music Lectures'.

[2] Rennert, *Crotch*, 43–7; Wollenberg, *Music at Oxford*, 39–40.

[3] Crotch, *Substance of Several Courses*, ed. Rainbow, v.

[4] For discussion of Crotch's lectures see Kassler, 'Royal Institution Music Lectures'; Irving, *Ancients and Moderns*, 11–18.

[5] Crotch, *Substance of Several Courses*.

[6] Duckles, 'Musicology', 484, 488.

continued into the 19th century, but it was the 'aesthetic' line that appealed more strongly to Romantic sensibilities.

Crotch had many successors. The pre-eminent English composer of his generation, Samuel Wesley, followed him at the Royal Institution, and offered revised forms of his lectures at various other venues. He was also influenced by Burney and Reynolds, and actively sought Burney's advice when preparing his first course in 1809. But, in the words of his biographer, his lectures 'show him in a stiffly formal and self-consciously learned vein. As might be expected from their titles, their subject matter was very general, and Wesley treated them as opportunities to ride various hobby-horses and to retail anecdotes in an overall structure that can only be described as rambling.'[1]

The formula of lectures read from a written text and varied by live illustrations proved to be extremely popular. It seems to have suited the temperament of English music lovers. As Duckles has said, 'Englishmen, in their thought about music, have always taken greater interest in the artistic than in the scientific aspect of their discipline. They have never ceased to regard music as a realm of concrete experience, not a field for philosophical speculation.'[2]

In 1806, following the pattern of the Royal Institution, the London Institution was founded 'for the Advancement of Literature and the Diffusion of Useful Knowledge'. A fine neo-classical building designed for its lectures and classes was erected at Finsbury Circus, Moorfields, in 1819. It sponsored 120 lectures on music between that date and 1854: among the speakers were Crotch, Wesley, Henry J. Gauntlett, Vincent Novello, Edward Taylor, Henry Bishop, and William H. Monk.[3] Taylor was also appointed professor of music at Gresham College from 1837, and was the first recent holder of that post to do his duty by offering a serious, methodical course of lectures. So by the time Sterndale Bennett was invited to lecture for the London Institution in 1857, the genre was well established. He could rely on a number of useful precedents, and his audiences would come to the lectures with well-formed expectations.

William Sterndale Bennett

William Sterndale Bennett (1816–75) may be regarded as the most distinguished composer of the early Victorian era, the only plausible rivals among his contemporaries being Samuel Sebastian Wesley (1810–76) and Michael William Balfe (1808–70). The lives and musical ideals of these

1 Olleson, *Samuel Wesley*, 85, 89, 188.
2 Duckles, 'Musicology', 484.
3 *Descriptive Catalogue of the Lectures Delivered at the London Institution*, 9, 62–3.

three musicians barely overlapped. Whereas Wesley in the end wrote mainly for the church and Balfe for the theatre, Bennett concentrated his efforts on instrumental music and domestic song. Wesley's audience was almost exclusively English, while Balfe turned to France and Italy for both his models and his international reputation. By contrast, Bennett's ideals were firmly focused on Germany.

He was educated and trained at the Royal Academy of Music. His seminal teacher there was Cipriani Potter (1792–1871), who had studied with Joseph Wölfl and (at Beethoven's suggestion) with Aloys Forster, and who made it his business to instruct his students in the forms and styles of the modern German instrumental school. Potter encouraged Bennett to write piano concertos in the classical form, and when he performed his first piano concerto at an Academy concert on 26 June 1833, Mendelssohn was in the audience. He asked to be introduced to the seventeen-year-old composer, and promptly invited him to Leipzig, not as a pupil but as a friend. Such a gesture from the man who was well on the way to becoming the idol of the English musical world must have had a hugely encouraging, even transforming effect on the diffident youth. He took up Mendelssohn's invitation in a brief visit in May 1836, and made several longer visits to Germany during the next six years for a total of over fourteen months. During this time he became a valued member of the lively musical circle of which Mendelssohn was the acknowledged leader, and, in particular, an intimate friend of Robert Schumann.[1] These were clearly the formative years of Bennett's life.

They were also the golden years of his achievement as a composer, when he created a series of masterpieces for orchestra, piano, and solo voice that gave promise of great things to come, and gained him a rare and enviable reputation in Germany. Although he continued to compose for the rest of his life, and could produce first-rate works on a grand scale, his productivity undoubtedly fell off. It is a matter of debate whether this was primarily due to a failure of self-confidence or to the pressure of all the other work that he was obliged to undertake to support his family.[2] But it is beyond doubt that Bennett devoted a large portion of his time to teaching, administration, and conducting. He was conductor of the Philharmonic Society (1855–66), professor of music at Cambridge (1856–75), and director of the Royal Academy of Music (1866–75), in addition to many occasional public duties. Far from treating such positions as honourable sinecures, Bennett, like the best of the Victorians, took all his duties extremely seriously. Most of all, he felt

1 See Bennett, *Life*, chaps. 4, 8; Temperley, 'Schumann and Sterndale Bennett', 207–10.
2 See Bennett, *Life*, 390–92; Temperley, 'Bennett'.

it an almost sacred obligation to pass on whatever wisdom he had acquired to later generations.[1]

The lectures that he gave in London, Sheffield, and Cambridge are an important part of that legacy. In them he was constrained to work out and encapsulate the views on musical matters that he no doubt expressed in less formal ways in his dealings with hundreds of students, fellow musicians, and lay persons. It is not surprising to find that his lectures reflect much the same opinions, influences, priorities, and beliefs as his compositions. When, for instance, he derided the sentimental ballads that were so widely disseminated, he had himself already taken pains to establish a serious English song culture along the lines of the German lied.[2] And when he condemned the prevalence of the so-called 'fantasia', which was little more than a medley of Italian opera songs,[3] he had already published a fantasia of his own which was an object-lesson in restoring the genre to the serious place it had occupied in the music of Mozart.[4] His criticisms (always expressed with moderation) of both contemporary Italian opera and the avant-garde German school led by Wagner paralleled his chosen path in composition, which was governed by a Brahms-like determination to demonstrate the continuing vitality and expressive power of classical forms and procedures.

Both as composer and as lecturer, Bennett was a strong musical patriot. But he was not a 'nationalist' in the sense of asserting recognisably English traits in his musical style. (Here he can be contrasted with his contemporary and schoolfellow, George Alexander Macfarren.[5]) On the contrary, he saw the salvation of English music in the adoption of German ways. As he said of the Germans, 'they enjoy music for itself and apart from display'.[6] He had modelled his own style on that of the great Germans from Bach to Mendelssohn, avoiding the perceived hazards of imitating the avant-garde of his day; and now he urged young English composers to do the same. His tastes were far from narrow. On the contrary, he shows a surprisingly cosmopolitan knowledge and sympathy, expressing (for instance) well-informed admiration for such widely differing composers as Purcell, Gluck, Grétry, Rossini, and Auber. He gave due credit to the English composers of the past. But there was never any doubt where his primary loyalties lay; and in his last lecture he chose Mozart as the ideal model for the contemporary student of composition.

1 Bennett, *Life*, 396–406.
2 See p. 41; also Temperley, 'Sterndale Bennett and the Lied'.
3 See p. 39.
4 For a full discussion see Yang, 'Bennett's Fantasia'.
5 See Temperley, 'Musical Nationalism'.
6 See p. 41.

Bennett never claimed to be a scholar or historian, and in dealing with historical matters he relied heavily on secondary sources, especially Charles Burney's *General History of Music* (1776–89) and George Hogarth's *Musical History, Biography, and Criticism* (1838) – which, in turn, was greatly influenced by Burney. One does not therefore look to Bennett for historical insights, and indeed many of the second- or third-hand conclusions he reached have long since been superseded. They do reveal the state of knowledge and opinion that was prevalent at the time and formed the basis of musical understanding. Like most writers, Bennett selected historical materials in part to bolster and confirm already-held opinions, and it is these opinions that are revealing to the modern reader. But there is no doubt that the most interesting passages for us today are those in which he discusses the music he knew well, and the musical conditions of his own time. Here he needed no secondary sources. He could draw directly on his natural musicality, his formidable experience, and his long considered opinions and feelings.

He developed a distinct philosophy that parallels and explains some of his personal decisions as a composer. Conscious of his rather lonely position as a leader in English musical life, he held strong convictions about his duty to the art of music and to his country, and strove to distil his experiences and principles for the guidance of younger musicians as well as consumers of music. He had learned that the path to achievement for an English composer was long, steep, and narrow, and he was concerned not only to impart courage to those who attempted it, but to warn them of the many pitfalls and hazards on either side. In addition he used his leading position in the English musical world to exhort and admonish the government and society at large to give more support to English music and musicians. The views he expresses cast much light on the aspirations of Victorian musicians as well as their inhibitions and prejudices, and help to explain the relative failure of Bennett himself, and of his British colleagues and contemporaries, to win permanent international success and acclaim for their music in a world that was moving on to newer things.

Lecturing could not be a high priority in Bennett's life. His regular teaching and administrative duties were burdensome, and barely provided him with an income adequate to support his family. He continually regretted that these obligations left him too little time to compose, especially in later life. It is very unlikely that he earned enough money from the lectures to compensate for the amount of time spent on their preparation. In the case of the Cambridge lectures, he was not paid at all.

In spite of all this, Bennett forced himself to prepare and deliver the lectures, hardly a congenial task for him. He must have had a powerful inner motivation. What was it? The evident answer is that he held a deep apprehension that music was in decline, especially in England, and felt that he had both the power and the duty to turn the situation around. As an acknowledged leader of his profession he might shame the government and wealthy individuals into providing more support and encouragement to professional musicians. As an admired composer and performer, he could demonstrate in practice the path that music should take to preserve its high aesthetic values, avoiding the pitfalls of sensationalism and the erosion of well-tried principles of form and tonality. And finally, as a teacher and lecturer he could encourage his hearers to strengthen the foundations of musicality in the home and in schools, and admonish composers to choose what he felt was the right path for the future of British music.

The London Lectures and their Audience

Bennett's lectures, with one exception, have never been published. The manuscripts survive in six bound volumes preserved by his family.[1] They are now in the possession of his great-great-grandson, Barry Sterndale-Bennett, at Longparish, Hampshire. From the surviving corpus of sixteen complete lectures and a few fragments, twelve have been selected for the present edition, all from the latter part of the composer's life, when he was ready to discourse in a reflective way on his ideas and experiences. Two earlier lectures, one for the newly founded Queen's College, London,[2] and the other for a London grammar school,[3] were designed for schoolchildren. They are of limited interest, apart from an occasional side comment, and they have not been included here.

In 1857 Bennett was asked to give a course of public lectures on music at the London Institution. It was announced as the last of ten courses offered for the 1857–58 season, the others being on art, philosophy, law, and a number of scientific and technological topics. Bennett's lectures were to be given on Thursdays, 8, 15, and 29 April and 6 May 1858, at 7 o'clock in the evening, and were announced simply as 'Four Lectures on Music'.[4]

The invitation was not only an honour but a considerable challenge, and it prompted Bennett to arrange his ideas in an orderly fashion. The

1 These are physically described in Williamson, *Bennett*, 191–6.

2 'On Harmony', in vol. 6 of the manuscript lectures, was delivered at Queen's College on 1 May 1848, and was published in revised form as one of a collection of *Introductory Lectures Delivered at Queen's College, London* (London: John W. Parker, 1849) by several authors including Charles Kingsley and F. D. Maurice.

3 'A Lecture on the Choice of Music', in vol. 5 of the manuscript lectures, was delivered at Maida Hill Grammar School on 12 June 1854.

4 Printed syllabuses are bound in with the manuscript lectures.

1. The London Institution: The Theatre, or Lecture Room

The site of Bennett's lectures in 1858 and 1864. A piano and several musicians had to be accommodated in the well. The building was erected in Finsbury Circus in 1819 and demolished in 1936.

decision to focus on music in England was his own rather than that of his hosts. He began his first lecture by saying: 'Having been engaged by the council of this institution to deliver four lectures on music, it appeared to me that I could not better employ the opportunity than by choosing those subjects which would immediately appeal to the sympathies of English amateurs, and of all those interested in the progress of music in this country.' In truth, however, most 'English amateurs' of the day were more likely to prefer foreign music.[1] His choice of topics was undoubtedly intended not only to steer their tastes towards a higher level, but also to draw their attention to the claims of English music.

The lectures were illustrated by live 'specimens' of music performed by Bennett with the help of a few students and colleagues. He borrowed the method and the term from Crotch. As he was considered an outstanding pianist by German as well as English critics, with 'exquisite

1 See Temperley, 'Xenophilia in English Musical History'.

tone and touch', his live illustrations must have greatly enhanced the effect of the lectures.[1]

The series was markedly successful. *The Musical World* reported as follows on 8 May 1858:

> LONDON INSTITUTION.—On Thursday evening Professor Bennett gave the last of a series of four highly instructive and entertaining lectures at this institution. The lectures were devoted to the following subjects:—No. 1. "On the State of Music in English Private Society." No. 2. "On the Visits of Illustrious Foreign Musicians to England." No. 3. "The Vocal Music of England." No. 4. "On the Future Prospects of England as a Musical Nation." On each occasion nearly 1,000 persons attended.[2]

The first two lectures were repeated at Sheffield, Bennett's birthplace, in the following year. This event will be discussed in the next section.

The London Institution asked him to deliver another series, but he did not find time to do so until six years later. This time the planned topic was an unexpected one: 'The Dramatic Music of France, Belgium, Germany, and Italy', later changed to 'On the Music for the Theatre Composed by Natives of Belgium, Italy, France, and Germany'.[3] The lectures were delivered on Monday evenings, 15 and 22 February, and 7 and 21 March 1864. As before, they were illustrated by musical 'specimens' in which Bennett was assisted by other performers.

Again he chose the subject himself,[4] though it is not possible to determine how far the wishes of the lecture committee of the Institution influenced his choice, since no records or correspondence on the matter have survived. He withheld a full explanation of his decision until near the end of the last lecture. Though it is not entirely coherent, his aim seems to have been to demonstrate that current trends in opera were undesirable, and that English composers would do well to keep away from the genre unless it was totally reformed: 'it will require the strong hand of a Scarlatti or Gluck to reduce this musical chaos to order'.[5] As in the first series, one often has the impression that he was really speaking to fellow professionals and critics, over the heads of the audience of amateur music-lovers for whom the series was ostensibly designed. He was also, however, much concerned about the influence his hearers might have on the coming generation. He made a direct appeal to parents and teachers, at the end of Lecture 3, to 'help the art & thereby the composers of

[1] O'Leary, 'Sir William Sterndale Bennett', 136.

[2] *Musical World* 36 (1858), 298. The audience estimate must have been an exaggeration, since the hall only accommodated 700 (Cutler, *London Institution*, 146).

[3] For an explanation of the change see the opening paragraphs of Lecture 5, p. 83.

[4] '. . . when invited to give the present course of lectures, the subject of opera music suggested itself to me as one of great interest in England at the present time' (see p. 124).

[5] See p. 124.

England to maintain that position to which . . . they are so justly entitled . . . . This can be done most effectively by the style of the music adopted in the education of those for whom you are responsible.' A similar motivation had lain behind his earlier 'Lecture on the Choice of Music' to Maida Hill Grammar School (not included here).

This series on 'Music for the Theatre' suffers from Bennett's relative inexperience in the world of opera and his lack of knowledge of its history. For the earlier history of opera there were virtually no scores that he could study or present as examples, outside the pages of Burney's *History* and Crotch's *Specimens*, unless he was prepared to conduct primary research in the manuscript collections of the larger libraries. Even if he had had time for such work, he was not particularly well equipped for it; few were in his time. His ignorance of early Italian opera is particularly clear in Lecture 6. Nevertheless, the second series was appreciated as much as the first. The London Institution asked for more.[1] Evidently he had a gift for conveying ideas about music to well-informed but non-specialist listeners. They respected his standing and his talents, and they were eager to hear what he had to tell them.

The *Musical World*, reporting on the first lecture, said that it 'afforded amusement and information in equal degrees to a highly intelligent audience'.[2] The *Musical Standard* inserted a short notice of the fourth lecture, showing a rather different assessment of the audience: 'The remarks of the learned lecturer were exceedingly brief, the illustrations being purposely made over prominent, we presume, to suit the very miscellaneous auditory thronging the theatre of this fine institution whenever a lecture on music is announced.'[3] This is a just criticism. Some parts of the text seem to be no more than a perfunctory introduction to the music that followed, where perhaps Bennett felt more confident of his ability to communicate his feelings and the character of the music. But as to the audience, he seems to have assumed that it was much the same as that which attended other courses of lectures at the London Institution.[4]

The Sheffield Lectures

In April 1859 the Sheffield Literary and Philosophical Society announced in the local papers that Bennett would deliver two lectures on music at the Music Hall on the evenings of Wednesday and Friday, 27 and 29

1 Bennett, *Life*, 333.
2 *Musical World* 42 (1864), 122.
3 *Musical Standard* 2 (1864), 277.
4 '. . . an audience so unaccustomed to anything but the real truth in art and science' (p. 38).

2. The Music Hall, Sheffield

Used for meetings of the Sheffield Literary and Philosophical Society (1822–1868). Here Bennett delivered two lectures in 1859. The building later housed the public library but was demolished in 1934 to make way for a new building.

April.[1] His fee was forty guineas (£42).[2] During his visit to Sheffield he stayed at the Victoria Hotel, Clarkehouse Road. It seems that the president of the society, E. Stirling Howard, was an old friend of Bennett's father Robert (1788–1819), who had been organist of the parish church before his early death.[3] The subjects, and in all essentials the texts, were the same as those of the first two London Institution lectures. Not surprisingly, the event was more newsworthy in the provincial city than it had been in the capital, and attracted considerable attention, coupled with pride in the fact that the lecturer was a native of Sheffield. A preview in the *Sheffield Daily Telegraph* is typical:[4]

> LECTURES ON MUSIC. — It will be seen from the advertisement that the council of our Literary and Philosophical Society have engaged Mr. Sterndale Bennett to give two lectures on music, a treat for which we doubt not the members will be truly grateful; for besides the anticipated gratification of such an interlude amidst the annual routine of instruction of a

1 *Sheffield and Rotherham Independent*, 9, 16, 23 April; *Sheffield Times*, *Sheffield Daily Telegraph*, 16 April onwards. Previous lectures on music had been given by Edward Taylor and Henry Bishop (Mackerness, *Somewhere Further North*, 32).

2 Freemantle, *Sterndale Bennett and Sheffield*, 122.

3 Freemantle, *Sterndale Bennett and Sheffield*, 119.

4 *Sheffield Daily Telegraph*, 20 April. See the same newspaper, 25 April; *Sheffield and Rotherham Independent*, 23 April; and *Sheffield Times*, 23 April.

> more ordinary, scientific, or literary character, the worthy professor in this case comes before a Sheffield audience with special attractions. He is, as most of our local readers are aware, a native of this town; and we need scarcely add, one of the most accomplished and respected composers, travellers [*sic*], and practitioners of music in England: we have, therefore, no doubt but that this rare opportunity of hearing Doctor Bennett give lectures and illustrations of the art with which his reputation is so widely and justly identified, will secure a large increase of subscribers to the institute.

Catering to local feeling, Bennett made a few changes in the texts of his lectures to mitigate their almost exclusive concentration on London events; for example, he added a reference to the Leeds and Bradford choral festivals. The musical illustrations were now moved to the end of the lectures, and the selections were quite different, no doubt in part because different performers were available. Percival Phillips, a local organist and former pupil of Bennett's, assisted at the piano; Miss Seale sang on the first evening, and Miss Clark and Mr Heathcote on the second; a 'choir', mentioned in early advertisements, did not materialise. On the first evening, Bennett introduced each piece of music with some further remarks.[1] Perhaps he felt able to command more time there than he had at the London Institution. Another possibility is that he thought the Sheffield audience needed a fuller explanation if they were to appreciate the music.

These lectures were not, strictly speaking, public. They were offered to members of the Society; 'proprietors' could bring three guests, 'subscribers' two, provided the guests were either 'Strangers, resident [at least] four miles from Sheffield, or Ladies or Young Men of their own families'.[2] Because of the prominence of the event in the Sheffield context, the local newspapers gave generous and almost entirely favourable reviews. In addition to summarising the contents of the lectures, they added a few comments from which we can glean information about the audience.

The *Sheffield Daily Telegraph* had pointed out in advance the duty of the affluent classes to support the lectures: 'it will be seen by the syllabus that the subject is to be treated in a way eminently calculated to arouse a spirit of inquiry, and to show the importance of the study of music in a national point of view, bearing as it does on the moral and social education of the people. We trust to see at these lectures a good attendance of the influential portion of our townsmen. They will derive much pleasure,

[1] Full details of the musical programmes and the introductory remarks are given in the Appendix.

[2] Proprietors were presumably shareholders; subscribers paid half a guinea a year. See *Sheffield Daily Telegraph*, 16 April 1859.

and see the necessity of countenancing all the efforts which are made to give a legitimate direction to the musical taste of the working population.' In reviewing the first lecture, the same paper noted the presence of 'a very large audience of the members and friends of the Literary and Philosophical Society.' It reserved its strongest praise for Bennett's playing, which 'delighted the audience'.[1]

The Sheffield Daily News and Evening Advertiser (28 April) went further: 'Though nominally a lecture, the oral part of the proceedings was comparatively insignificant, [the] great attraction being a selection of music, the principal portions of which were exquisitely rendered by Mr. Bennett himself. . . The audience, which was numerous, was of a highly intellectual and appreciative character, and were greatly delighted with the selection of standard classical music which was so admirably presented.' Similar, though shorter, reviews were printed in response to the second lecture.

However, the 'highly intellectual and appreciative character' of the audience is brought into question by a pair of letters to the editor of the *Telegraph*. 'A Subscriber' wrote that at the first lecture he was 'unfortunately very near to some ladies, who kept up a running conversation during the performance of even the most beautiful music in the programme'. He went on:

> A gentleman said to me, before I attended the lecture, "Playing Bach's hand fugues [*sic*] in Sheffield will be casting pearls before swine." I scarcely thought that was a just remark respecting the members of the Sheffield Literary and Philosophical Society; but am sorry to say that a great deal of the pleasure that I should have experienced during the exquisite performance of the first movement of Beethoven's "Moonlight Sonata," and also Mendelssohn's "Andante" and "Rondo Capriccioso," was prevented by such refined remarks as the following: "Well, what plaintive ditties!" "He looks like a Methodist parson!" (The speaker was evidently not a Methodist.) "Are you taking the music all in?" "It may be very grand!" "I couldn't tell the difference between his playing and our Fanny's!" "Is that dress silk?" "She wants another hoop higher up!" "What a gay bonnet Miss —— has got on!" &c.

It seems that the talking took place during the music rather than the lectures. The writer hoped that such behaviour would not, on the second evening, 'inflict such a punishment on those who wish to profit by the opportunity, so rarely afforded in Sheffield, of hearing the delightful playing of Dr. Bennett.'[2]

There was a response next day from 'Amy', who, while agreeing with

1 *Sheffield Daily Telegraph*, 20, 28 April 1859.

2 *Sheffield Daily Telegraph*, 29 April 1859.

A Subscriber's strictures on the talkers, asked why he did not also censure the 'gentlemen' who congregated near the doors of the hall: 'many an exquisite passage was lost to us through their audible remarks'. 'Certainly,' she pointed out, 'such talkative gentlemen cannot go to admire the music. What then can be their object? Is it because they fancy it rather "the thing" to be there seen? To criticise the ladies and each other?'[1]

Several studies have shown that the early Victorian period was one in which the convention of silence during the performance of serious music was slowly becoming established.[2] A prime influence in this direction was John Ella's Musical Union, which from its foundation in 1845 carried a motto on its programmes: '*Il più grand' omaggio alla musica sta nel silenzio*'.[3] These studies have chiefly investigated the situation in London; it seems likely that provincial cities had not yet fully caught up with the new attitudes, yet the tone of the two letters suggests that pressure against talking during music was beginning to grow.

The Cambridge Lectures

On 4 March 1856 Bennett was elected professor of music at Cambridge by a large majority of the Senate, in succession to Thomas Attwood Walmisley (1814–56). The post was unpaid and enjoyed little prestige within the university,[4] and there was no course of study in music at the time; the Faculty of Music was not established until 1947. Nevertheless Walmisley had, on his own initiative, delivered lectures on music which had been much appreciated. In his letter of application Bennett had written:

> In addition to the fulfilment of the ordinary duties attached to the Profes-sor-ship, which are understood to include the Setting to Music of the Installation Odes [of chancellors of the university], the Examination of Exercises for Degrees in Music, and the Direction of University Musical performances, it would be my wish to give an annual course of Lectures, which lectures (having the advantage of Illustration) should comprehend the rise, progress, and principles of Music, the Biography of Musicians, their various styles, and their influence in the different epochs of the art.[5]

1 *Sheffield Daily Telegraph*, 30 April 1859.

2 See, for instance, Temperley, 'Instrumental Music', 8–10, 28–30; Bashford, 'Learning to Listen'; Hall-Witt, 'Representing the Audience', 121 (n.1), 136.

3 'The greatest homage to music is silence.' For discussion see Bashford, 'John Ella', 208–10.

4 See Winstanley, *Unreformed Cambridge*, 142–3.

5 Cambridge University Library, UA CUR 39.10.1. The same archive contains printed

The volume of Bennett's Cambridge lectures contains the text of six discourses. The first of these, on 'Music Professorships', may have been an inaugural lecture addressed to an assembly of dons, perhaps in the Senate House. It has not been included here; the largely factual, historical information it contains is now accessible in more accurate forms. The others were addressed to practical musicians, especially those who aspired to become composers, as Bennett himself made clear.[1] One of these, on 'Instruments of the Orchestra', conveys elementary information only. The remaining four, however, are rich in Bennett's personal philosophy, and form Lectures 9–12 in this volume.

Whether he fulfilled his undertaking to give an 'annual course of lectures' may be doubted. He spent only a few days at Cambridge in most years. One might expect that he would have been particularly conscientious in the earlier years of his tenure of the chair, but if so, no texts survive from this early period. The annual University Calendar contains a brief entry under 'Professor of Music', but without any mention of lectures, though the lectures of other professors are listed; presumably, lectures on music were not considered of sufficient importance to be noticed. It is of course possible that Lectures 1–4, offered to the London Institution in 1858, had previously been delivered in some form at Cambridge in 1856 or 1857, though there is nothing to confirm it in the manuscript. The same might be true of Lectures 5–8.

Lectures 9–12, however, seem to be a planned series. The opening of Lecture 9 ('I purpose in my first lecture this term to begin at the very beginning') suggests that he was speaking to students.[2] What term was it? Lectures 11 and 12 are dated 4 February and 4 March 1871 respectively (both Saturdays). It seems likely that Bennett went up to Cambridge on four Saturdays during the Lent term, 1871, choosing Saturdays because he was too busy during the week with teaching and administering the Royal Academy of Music.[3]

letters of application from three other candidates, William R. Propert, Charles Edward Horsley, and Edward Dearle. All offered to give lectures, but Horsley only did so in a second, subsidiary letter, possibly after his supporters in the Senate had told him about Bennett's offer: 'Since I had the honour of forwarding to you my Address accompanying my Testimonials, it has been represented to me that it will be advisable to state my intention, should I obtain the appointment of Professor of Music, to deliver Lectures on the History and Practice of the Art, at such times as may be in accordance with the rules of the University.'

1 See p. 155.

2 Although there was no formal course in music at the university, no doubt there were students and others who wished to learn something about the craft of composition.

3 The Lent term in 1871 lasted from 13 January to 31 March (*Cambridge University Calendar*, xxxiii–xxxv). No record of the lectures has been found in the university archives; likely dates for Lectures 9 and 10 are Saturdays 14, 21, or 28 January. Two

3. The Arts School, Cambridge University
A medieval courtyard now called the Old Schools. The west range (left), completed in 1457, housed the room later known as the Arts School, which contained a 'Pulpit for the professor'. Here Bennett delivered lectures in 1871 and probably earlier.

Some aspects of the Cambridge lectures suggest that Bennett was consciously summing up his ideas and passing on a final legacy to the musicians of a younger generation. Indeed, he began Lecture 12 with an explicit appeal to 'those studying music with a view to obtain any eminence in the art' and continued by asking which of the great composers should be models for young composers of the day.

But how many aspiring composers are likely to have been among his Cambridge hearers? One such was Charles Villiers Stanford, who entered Cambridge as an eighteen-year-old undergraduate in October 1870, and who late in life would publish a warm tribute to Sterndale Bennett as an inspiration of his youth.[1] He met the professor only by chance during one of Bennett's brief visits to the university. He was much moved at being in the presence of a man whose compositions he had

pieces of internal evidence confirm that these two undated lectures were given at least no earlier than the late 1860s: Bennett's words about Wagner's reception in Germany ('Night after night the same opera and the same audience! and the same deep and mysterious approbation!' – p. 130) and his treatment of Rossini as someone already dead (p. 139).

1 Stanford, 'William Sterndale Bennett'.

known and loved since boyhood. 'Over it all was the consciousness of a compelling artistic atmosphere which idealised the man from whom it emanated. It came not only from the many and great associations which his presence recalled, but from his own innate nobility.'[1] Later, Bennett strongly supported the young man's performing activities in Cambridge. Yet he did not become his teacher. Stanford had already decided that England could not provide him with adequate training as a composer. He planned to study in Germany. In his memoir of Bennett, he did not mention the lectures of 1871 and may not even have attended them, though he was apparently in Cambridge at the time. As Jeremy Dibble points out, 'Bennett was, in Stanford's opinion, the country's leading composer, but, just as Parry had discovered, his lack of sympathy with anything contemporary rendered him unsuitable as a critical teacher.'[2]

The series of professional musicians who received degrees at Bennett's hands included few who ever resided in Cambridge, and none who (as far as can be discovered) wrote memoirs in which Bennett's lectures might have been mentioned.[3] Thus no contemporary reactions to the Cambridge lectures have been found. Whatever the listeners' response may have been, the university authorities evidently approved. Bennett was voted a £100 annual stipend in 1867 on the grounds that 'his services could not with propriety remain any longer unrequited'.[4] In the same year he was awarded an honorary MA, which made him a member of the Senate. And when, after his death, he was succeeded by George Alexander Macfarren, the letter of appointment stipulated, for the first time, 'that the Professor be required to give a course of not less than four lectures in Music annually at the university.'[5] If Bennett came anywhere close to that ideal, the records are lost.

In the Cambridge lectures Bennett reached his high point. He spoke with greater freedom and boldness in the university surroundings. This was where he gave final expression to long-held views, often on matters he had only touched on in earlier lectures. Without the distraction of frequent musical illustrations he was free to explore questions in greater depth. He no longer felt any compulsion to mention composers of whom he knew very little and cared less. He spoke instead of the kinds of music

1 Stanford, 'William Sterndale Bennett', 628.

2 Dibble, *Stanford*, 58.

3 Between 1856 and 1874 twenty men earned the Cambridge degree of bachelor of music and eleven that of doctor of music (see Williams, *Short Account*, 143–5). At least one of these, Joseph Parry (1841–1903), was a pupil of Bennett's at the Royal Academy of Music from 1868 to 1871, but it is unlikely that he attended his lectures at Cambridge.

4 Bennett, *Life*, 363.

5 Banister, *George Alexander Macfarren*, 320.

that he loved most, and expounded on issues where his feelings were strong enough to breach his customary reserve.

Character of the Lectures

What of Bennett's personal style as a lecturer? It appears that he followed the normal practice of the day by reading directly from a written text, though there are a few marginal comments that suggest an occasional impromptu 'aside'. By all accounts, his demeanour was distinguished, his voice persuasive, but he was modest and reserved in his manner. In the lectures he too frequently disclaims expertise and hedges his stronger statements with qualifications. William Spark's judgment of his personality is telling: 'He was always shy and reticent, and so gentle and refined in his manners and conduct as to become a perfect model to the swarms of self-sufficient, arrogant "professors" who now unfortunately occupy prominent positions in the art world of music, without being in the least deserving thereof.'[1] But he was also known for his vivacity and for a quiet sense of humour.[2]

His son and biographer said that 'his voice was singularly expressive, and he had an excellent delivery,' but considered that 'his opinions . . . on music and musicians were given with his habitual restraint, and for that reason the lectures, which he left in manuscript, are unsatisfying. They give the impression that he often checked himself just as he was on the verge of letting out something very interesting. There are sentences scratched out which confirm this impression.'[3] Indeed, the lectures are often as interesting for what they leave out as for what they say.

It must be admitted that Bennett was no master of verbal expression of the order of Robert Schumann or Hector Berlioz. He was never a music critic, nor did he write substantially for publication. There are many indications that the task of writing did not come easily to him, and that he had to exert a strong effort of will to induce himself to undertake it. His word choices and order are sometimes awkward. Parts of the lectures are actually written in his wife's hand (see Plate 4); some of these are copied from books, others no doubt dictated by Bennett or copied from his rough notes.

Neither was he a seasoned public speaker, and there are signs of inexperience in the design of the lectures, in some anomalous or ambiguous

1 W. Spark, *Musical Memories*, 129.

2 Bennett, *Life*, 423–39.

3 Bennett, *Life*, 333. Many of these deletions have been deciphered and recorded in this edition, as well as a few scribbled notes that indicate preliminary ideas. See also the rejected introduction to Lecture 4: p. 68, n.1.

21.

Time will not allow me to give you many specimens of that remarkable era in English Music when flourished our great Madrigal writers — Quoting from Hogarth's Musical History,

Most of the great Italian ~~writers~~ Composers of the sixteenth Century distinguished themselves by their Madrigals; particularly Palestrina, Luca Marenzio, Giovanni Croce, Stradella, Steffani and others — About the period of which we speak, the madrigals of these Composers began to be adapted to English words and thus the foundation was laid for a school in which we soon rivalled, if not surpassed, the Italians themselves.

These beautiful productions, in the age in which they appeared, were the music chiefly resorted to as a recreation in England. To sing in parts was an accomplishment held to be indispensable in a well educated Lady or gentleman.

At a Social meeting, when the madrigal books were laid on the table, everybody was expected to take a share in the harmony; and any one who declined on the score of inability, was looked upon with some contempt, as rude & low-bred.

4. Part of the text of Lecture 3 (see p. 58).

The upper half of the page is written by Bennett, making corrections as he went along. The lower half was written by Mary Bennett, possibly from her husband's dictation.

turns of phrase, and in the platitudes and superfluous apologies which sometimes clutter the text. He evidently did not have all the material in his head, and had to research his facts in contemporary printed sources. He would only speak after extensive rehearsal, with his friend George Hogarth serving as listener and critic.[1]

The quality that comes through most strongly in the lectures is unselfishness. Although Bennett was hard up for money for most of his life, there is no sign of any attempt to promote his own work, or to curry favour with either the public or the powerful. He never boasted. He avoided saying anything that might even have the appearance of self-congratulation, as when he declined to claim special knowledge of Mendelssohn's private character.[2] He clearly took little pleasure in criticising colleagues and contemporaries;[3] indeed, he made it a point of principle to treat foreign composers with respect.[4] But he did not shrink from criticism when he felt the need to give warning of the danger they represented. One is never in doubt that he was working for the general good as he saw it, and for the future of his art, especially in his own country. Whatever economic forces might be shaping the course of musical history, he, for one, was not giving in to them. He could indeed speak with passion on subjects close to his heart, as he did in the closing paragraphs of Lecture 1 (p. 43) and in the Cambridge lectures.

Bennett's Goals and Views

His primary concern, then, was the state of music in England. He assailed foreign critics for ignoring English music in their writings, which he contrasted with England's generous welcome to foreign musicians.[5] He reminded his listeners of the glories of England's musical past and the continuing excellence of her vocal music (Lecture 3). He praised the progress in both performing standards and appreciation of good music that had occurred in England in the last two generations.[6] In Lecture 1, however, his opening question is tinged with irony: '"Is England a musical nation?" My first idea of an answer to this question has been "Who can doubt it?" What country pays more for music than England?'[7]

1 Bennett, *Life*, 333.
2 See p. 56.
3 Contrast, for example, his own mild reservations about contemporary Italian opera with the blunt remarks of Hogarth that he then quotes: p. 34.
4 See p. 68.
5 See p. 69.
6 See pp. 32, 57.
7 See p. 32.

He goes on to outline the astonishing variety of London's public musical life in concerts and operas, giving credit where it is due. But his next question uncovers his real message: ' "What is done for music at home?" '[1] And here he has to admit that England has much to learn from Germany. He knows the secret of Germany's musical primacy from his own experience: Germans really love good music, and play it in their own homes as a matter of course, whereas in England musical performances are social and commercial events. He concludes: 'That England has the power to become a really "musical nation" no one can deny. That it is at present fully deserving that title I dare not venture to affirm.'

He frequently returns to this idea in later lectures, and it underlies much of his historical discussion, which tends to exalt what we call the Classical period as a golden age from which the decline is already far advanced, even in Germany. At the end of Lecture 4 he even suggests that the relative lack of support for composers in England has the advantage of preventing them from joining the radical changes of style taking place in Germany. Lecture 9 is the most pessimistic, a jeremiad in which he condemns Wagner's operas and the Crystal Palace Handel festivals alike, on the grounds that they cannot be reduced to the domestic scale which was for him the true gauge of musical health.

This belief in preserving an intimate scale for music leads him to some conclusions that are in a sense prophetic, looking beyond the gargantuan excesses of 1900 to the early music movement of the late 20th century. He doubts the wisdom of the 'additional accompaniments' that were normally added to Handel's scores; he expresses concern that mechanical improvements to instruments and the historical rise in pitch may distort old compositions.[2] He even predicts that one day Handel's operas will be revived on stage. Ernest Walker in 1907 was still talking of 'the virtual impossibility of staging nowadays an entire Handelian opera in its original shape';[3] yet by the end of the 20th century every one of them had been successfully staged. It is also true, of course, that Haydn and Mozart, after a period of relative neglect, would be more fully appreciated once again in the later 20th century, reinforcing Bennett's view that they represented a pinnacle of musical history. Mendelssohn also, after a long decline, is in the process of rehabilitation, even if he may never again occupy the pinnacle of esteem at which Bennett and his English contemporaries would have placed him.

Bennett made his own contributions to musicology. He revived works from the 'London pianoforte school' in his series *Classical Practice*

1 See p. 38.
2 See pp. 131, 132.
3 Walker, *A History of Music in England*, 191.

(1839–47), edited Handel's *Acis and Galatea* for the Handel Society (1847), revived the *St Matthew Passion* (1854) and other works of Bach for the London Bach Society, which he founded, and edited German chorales for *The Chorale Book for England* (1863).[1]

His conviction, shared by most Europeans of his time (outside Italy), was that the great Germans from Bach to Mendelssohn had laid the foundation for all that was best in music, and should be the principal models for those who sought a national revival. He was undoubtedly strengthened in this view by his long visits to Germany as a young man and by his personal friendship with Mendelssohn and his circle. He was profoundly disturbed by current trends of the 'Music of the Future', but he hesitated to condemn Liszt and Wagner outright; instead, he gave them perfunctory acknowledgment, or omitted them altogether from discussion. He did the same with Berlioz and Verdi. He never mentioned Schubert or Chopin at all. He was clearly ambivalent about the music of Schumann, which he could not wholeheartedly admire even though the composer had been his close personal friend and beer-drinking companion.[2] On the other hand, unlike Schumann, he was surprisingly enthusiastic about Rossini and the contemporary composers of French grand opera.

The positive side to Bennett's lectures lay in his genuine and unstinted admiration for the great German composers, above all Mendelssohn, who for him was the last of them. Here his heart and mind could pull together in the same direction, and he could shed his habitual caution, saying of Mendelssohn: 'His genius was universal. He was grand in all departments of the art, & as a man, most lovable. . . The grand fact will ever remain that he wrote for England the "Elijah".'[3] Unexpectedly, he reserved the ultimate tribute for Weber: 'I have no hesitation in pronouncing him one of the greatest geniuses we have ever known, if not the greatest.'[4]

But in his final lecture, after considering all the great names, he concluded that Mozart, not Mendelssohn or Weber, was the best possible model for the aspiring composer. He said his choice was the product of 'deep conviction resulting from a careful study of all the characteristics, temperaments, habits of working, self denial of public applause, commercial gain, hasty ambition, and many other conflicting influences to be found in the history of great musicians.' It will be seen that his judgment of composers included moral criteria as well as artistic ones, and this typically Victorian position is found at several points in his discourse.

1 For details see Williamson, *Bennett*, 497–511.

2 For further evidence of this see Temperley, *Schumann and Sterndale Bennett*, 213–16.

3 See p. 56.

4 See p. 121.

In this light, his comments on Mozart's operas can only be called astounding. In the lecture 'On the Music for the Theatre Composed by Natives of Germany' he allotted less space to Mozart than to Handel or Gluck, and hardly more than to Haydn. The stated reason was a lame one: 'It will not be necessary for me to press the claims of Mozart upon your notice or to say many words upon his music.' But the only specimen he chose for illustration was a comic trio from *Die Entführung*, which he wrongly stated was written when Mozart was 'fourteen or fifteen', and he declared that 'The grandest and most dramatic of all the works of Mozart are unquestionably the "Idomeneo" and the "Clemenza di Tito" ' – Mozart's two mature examples of *opera seria*, neither of which was in the normal repertory at the time. No mention of *Le nozze di Figaro*, *Don Giovanni*, *Così fan tutte*, or even 'The Magic Flute'!

A possible reason for this startling omission is one that may also explain Bennett's general ambivalence toward opera. He was a 'Victorian' in the stereotypical sense: a prude. He could not wholeheartedly admire a drama that openly presented adultery and promiscuous sex and treated them as a subject for entertainment, as da Ponte and Mozart did. Possible support for this inference comes from his observation about Halévy's *La Juive*: that it had been 'performed in London, with a degree of success which was only qualified by the story being entirely unsuitable to the English public.'[1] The same feeling may well have been a strong though unspoken factor in his disapproval of Verdi and Wagner. But it cannot account for his warm admiration for the French school in general: 'Nothing in the art of the present day can compare in freshness and completeness with the Modern French Opera from the time of Boieldieu, Auber and Hérold.'[2] Evidently Bennett was conflicted on the matter. He felt he had to give composers their due if he could admire their genius and mastery, but sometimes the compliments stuck in his throat when he recalled the subject matter of some their operas.

Another contradiction about Mozart appears when he says that 'it has been remarked by more than one, that the tone of his comic operas is far too sombre . . . certainly we find some very serious airs and concerted music in situations which scarcely seem to justify them.' This comment came just after he had performed the boisterous trio 'Marsch, marsch,

1 See p. 110. In this opera, the supposedly Jewish heroine, Rachel, carries on a secret love affair with a Christian prince who pretends to be Jewish. In the dénouement it is revealed that she is not, as was supposed, the daughter of a Jewish goldsmith, but of a Christian cardinal, who has just condemned her to death. Of course it may have been the religious/ ethnic rather than the sexual features of this plot that Bennett considered 'unsuitable'.

2 See p. 105.

marsch' from *Die Entführung*.[1] It was certainly influenced by his friend and mentor, Hogarth, who developed the same notion, claiming that Mozart 'could raise a smile, but not laughter'.[2] But it tends to undermine Bennett's own remarks in Lecture 1: '. . . does it . . . follow that high class music is necessarily sombre . . . Cannot Mozart and Haydn be joyous . . .?'[3]

Since Bennett, near the end of his career, recommended Mozart as a model for young composers, it is natural to ask whether he had followed this advice in his own youth. His very early string quartet (1831) certainly shows a strong Mozartian influence, as do his first two symphonies (1832, 1833), and his devotion to Mozart was known to his schoolmates.[4] In his mature music one is not often reminded of Mozart by any superficial resemblances (one such is the opening of the G Minor Symphony of 1864, recalling that of Mozart's great symphony in the same key). Generally his turn of phrase, harmonic sense, and keyboard texture are all profoundly different. The most durable evidence for Mozart's influence is to be found in his structural principles. In the first movements of his piano concertos, for instance, he always followed the Mozartian form, including the full opening tutti, which many contemporaries, including Mendelssohn, were beginning to dispense with.[5] And he continued to use a variety of sonata-allegro form in many of his shorter piano pieces.

Bennett's belief in Mozart as a structural model may have come from his most important composition teacher. As already mentioned, Cipriani Potter had based his teaching on the Viennese classics, and on Mozart in particular. He gave the London premiere of several of Mozart's piano concertos and edited all his music for piano solo.[6] A contemporary pupil, George Alexander Macfarren, said that Potter 'showed his pupils the art of continuity in the development of musical ideas – the structure of complete compositions. I believe that this was not known in England before his time, or, if known, it was certainly unpractised.'[7] Possibly Bennett's advice to students was directly based on Potter's advice to him.

It is surprising to find that Bennett's feelings about Beethoven were at best equivocal. He conceded his greatness whenever the name came up, and especially praised the power of his 'instrumental dramatic

1 See p. 120.
2 Hogarth, *Musical History*, 106.
3 See p. 40.
4 Bennett, *Life*, 22–4.
5 For Bennett's comment on this, see Lecture 10, p. 142. For further discussion see Temperley, 'Mozart's Influence on English Music', 316–17.
6 Peter and Rushton, 'Potter'.
7 Banister, *Macfarren*, 23.

music';[1] but in writing of the string quartet he included Beethoven's name only as an afterthought. Perhaps he had reservations about the late quartets, as did many contemporaries. It is certainly true that in the programmes of his Classical Chamber Concerts (1843–56) he included only early- and middle-period works of Beethoven, by contrast with the Beethoven Quartett Society (founded by Thomas Alsager in 1845) which systematically performed all the quartets.[2] In Lecture 9 he criticised contemporaries for taking Beethoven's Ninth Symphony as a starting point for their own work: he may have been thinking of the symphonies of Berlioz and Schumann, or even Brahms's First Piano Concerto (1853). Clearly he deprecated any move, even by Beethoven, that tended to disrupt the pure classical forms of Mozart, and feared its consequences for the future. But he had no reserve in admiring the enhanced lyrical feeling that a composer such as Weber or Mendelssohn could invest in the classical forms, by means of advances in melodic and harmonic style or orchestration, or by expressive word-setting.

His devotion to classical forms was not unquestioning, however. In discussing 'Fashions in Music' he condemned the repeat of the exposition in sonata form, the da-capo aria, the *stretta* aria coda, and even the long orchestral tutti of the classical concerto, though he conceded that some of Mozart's tuttis 'are some of the finest imaginations of a man who could indeed "imagine".'[3] He commended Beethoven and Mendelssohn for omitting the opening tutti in some concertos, though, as already pointed out, he himself had observed it in his own full-length concertos, all of which were written under the direct tutelage or strong influence of Potter.[4]

Although by no means learned in musical history, Bennett did make some striking historical judgments regarding music he knew well. One of his Cambridge lectures is an astute comparison of Bach and Handel, in which he attributes many differences in their styles to the external circumstances of their lives. He also seems to anticipate the course of musical taste in the 20th century when he points to the already widening divergence between antiquarianism and radical modernism:

> As further distinct evidence of the conflict and agitation now going on, it can be pointed out that while on the one hand the effusions of the ultra German school, which deeply affect young students here and elsewhere,

1 See p. 87.

2 Programmes in the Bennett Library, Longparish; Bennett, *Life*, 211; programmes of the Beethoven Quartett Society, British Library, d. 54; *Musical World* 25 (1850), 297. For further discussion see Bashford, 'The Late Beethoven Quartets and the London Press'.

3 See p. 142.

4 He did, however, write a Caprice for piano and orchestra without an orchestral introduction, and he praised Weber for his *Konzertstück*, which also lacks an orchestral tutti.

appear so rapidly: on the other hand, societies are formed for the production in a splendid form of the works of the old & great masters, many of which have not before been published.[1]

Another thoughtful reading of musical history is the distinction he made among the greatest composers between pioneers and disciples. Alessandro Scarlatti, Gluck, and Haydn were pioneers; Mozart, Spohr, and Mendelssohn were disciples.[2] These historical positions may or may not have originated with Bennett, but they certainly show his intelligence and depth of understanding, and would be endorsed by most modern musicologists, who can make use of far wider knowledge and research.

Other judgments of Bennett's can only be regarded as eccentric. In dealing with Italian opera in Lecture 6 he made only the barest mention of Bellini, Donizetti, or Verdi, yet in his coverage of German opera in Lecture 8 he deemed it worth while to discuss works by Winter, Hummel, and even Himmel. And his undue attention to Belgian composers for the theatre (which was in part a consequence of unfortunate decisions in the design of the second London series[3]) led him to the unfathomable conclusion that 'if any new school of opera music should arise, it will come from Belgium and compete with France in individuality'.[4]

The evident reason for his disproportionate attention to Belgium was his admiration for the Belgian government's generous treatment of the country's musicians, especially through the Conservatoire Royale de Musique, directed by Fétis and Gevaert, which admitted all students free of charge. 'All power to Belgium – to the king, and to the government, who thus set an example to the rest of the world in the encouragement of musical art.'[5] He reasoned that with such advantages Belgium was well placed to take the lead in the musical world. He had already discussed this matter in the previous series, also praising Holland for its unique society for the furtherance of music, and France for its national

1 See p. 134.

2 See p. 135. In the next lecture he extended the list of 'guides' (= pioneers?) with the names of 'Bach, Handel, . . . — and (the name may sound strange) Rossini', but implied that Beethoven and Weber were in the 'disciple' class (p. 145).

3 His decision to classify the national schools of opera by the composers' place of birth led to inevitable distortions, and required a lecture on Belgium in order to accommodate Grétry. Bennett therefore padded out the very thin material on Belgian opera, first by using the first half of Lecture 5 for his general introduction to opera history, and then by devoting time to the relatively insignificant composers Fétis, Hannsens, and Gevaert (explained on p. 89).

4 See p. 94. This was no passing aberration; it was reinforced at the end of the series: 'you will remember that I expressed my idea that should any new school of dramatic music now arise, it will come from Belgium' (p. 123).

5 See p. 94.

conservatory.[1] Behind this praise was the bitterness he felt about the lack of national support in Britain, where music was left to the mercies of the free market. His indignation about this erupts at several points in the lectures, and would be redoubled by his own discouraging experiences when he petitioned for government relief for the failing finances of the Royal Academy of Music.[2] He also compared the plight of British music with the strong support enjoyed by the visual arts through the Royal Academy of Art.[3]

Whether Bennett was praising the Germans' thriving domestic music-making or the public support of musicians in the Low Countries and France, his underlying agenda was to change British habits and attitudes in ways that would lead to a national musical revival. From our vantage point we can see that the revival was already under way, even if it did not fully arrive in his time. But he could not see it coming, because it was not based on the classical principles he espoused. Here is what he said on the subject in Lecture 9:

> In fact nationality or individuality in music is fast disappearing, & perhaps altogether this is not to be regretted. Let it not be understood that I am referring to national songs, which I sincerely hope nations may keep. This may be considered a sarcastic wish since those people[s] who possess national songs in most abundance are the least educated in art.

'National songs', or folk songs, would be one of the pillars of the 'English Musical Renaissance', when they were indeed embraced by composers 'educated in art' such as Stanford and Vaughan Williams. The other pillars would be the rediscovery of Elizabethan and Jacobean music, with which Bennett had only moderate sympathy, and the influence of the advanced German school led by Wagner, with which he had none.

Yet it is easy to sympathise with his feelings and opinions, which are honestly expressed and not at all self-serving. As in his compositions, the strength of his convictions is heard not in bombastic self-assertion but in the loving care with which he sought to preserve and nourish the best of the European canon. The changes he opposed so resolutely, but could not prevent, would eventually lead to a musical culture in which progress and originality were overvalued against accumulated tradition. Although his conservative aesthetic would soon be swept aside, it is difficult to assert that it was wrong in itself. The composers Bennett most admired still form the core of our musical heritage, in spite of all that has happened since his time.

1 See p. 73.
2 Bennett, *Life*, 369–74.
3 See p. 78.

PART ONE

Lectures at London and Sheffield, 1858–1859

On Music in England

1

On the State of Music in English Private Society and the General Prospects of Music in the Future

London Institution, 8 April 1858
Sheffield Literary and Philosophical Society, 27 April 1859

Having been engaged by the council of this institution to deliver four lectures on music, it appeared to me that I could not better employ the opportunity than by choosing those subjects which would immediately appeal to the sympathies of English amateurs,[1] and of all those interested in the progress of music in this country.

Under this feeling, I have, for this evening's lecture, selected a theme which I have long had at heart, viz. an enquiry into 'the state of music in English private society'. For my second lecture, I propose to bring before you a subject which I trust you will find of the greatest interest, viz. the influence upon the progress of music in this country caused by the visits of illustrious foreign musicians to England from Handel to Mendelssohn.

On the third evening, I shall endeavour to do justice to those of our own countrymen to whom our gratitude is due for their masterly and melodious contributions to the vocal music of England, and my concluding lecture will be devoted to a speculation upon the chances of English music and English musicians in the future.

I have already said that my subject of this evening, viz. 'the state of music in English private society' as distinguished from music to be found in English concert halls, is one which I have very much at heart.

1 The word 'amateur' at this date still retained something of its older, positive sense of an aristocratic patron and knowledgable music-lover, rather than simply an untrained performer. See Gillett, 'Ambivalent Friendships'.

How often have I been startled at the question 'Is England a musical nation?' My first idea of an answer to this question has been 'Who can doubt it?' What country pays more for music than England? Note the strides which music has made within the last thirty years. Consider the time when the Philharmonic Society (happily still existing!) and the Ancient Concerts did all the work of art in public performance, saving the music heard at the benefit concerts of a few eminent professors,[1] who annually gathered their friends and pupils around them for the purpose of exhibiting their powers in those branches of performance for which they were celebrated.[2]

Now look around and remark the increasing thirst for public music in London and elsewhere. See the gigantic choral societies now in full work, each employing its half thousand amateur choristers and instrumentalists – performances night after night, performances which some few years back would have required a twelvemonth's preparation even of the details of arrangement.

The increase of the number of these large choral societies by no means seems to exhaust the supply of amateur performers. Thus the Sacred Harmonic Society is fully peopled. The London Sacred Harmonic Society maintains its hundreds. The Bach Society (an institution in which I confess myself to be deeply interested, it having for its object the bringing forward the long neglected works of the illustrious John Seb. Bach) also presents its 300 enthusiasts, all singing with heart and soul in honour of their patron. There is then the choir so admirably disciplined by Mr Leslie, for the performance of works belonging to a more sensitive class. Add to these the 'Vocal Association' presided over by Mr Benedict, the Polyhymnian Choir, the madrigal societies, and last not least the great vocal schools of Mr Hullah, and you have in London alone a mass of musical material reflecting the highest credit upon the enthusiasm and zeal of English amateurs.[3]

[1] That is, professional musicians.

[2] This must allude to the years from 1813, when the Philharmonic Society was founded, to about 1828. Bennett himself came to London as a student of the Royal Academy of Music in 1826, at the age of nine. The Concerts of Ancient Music continued until 1848.

[3] The Sacred Harmonic Society, founded by Joseph Surman in 1832, performed ten to a dozen oratorios at Exeter Hall each year under Michael Costa, who had replaced Surman when he was dismissed as conductor in 1848. Surman began a rival organisation, the London Sacred Harmonic Society, in that year (*Musical World* 23 (1848), 394, 406, 470, 725). The Bach Society was founded in 1849 with Bennett as chairman, and had given the first English performances of the *St Matthew Passion* under his direction at St. Martin's Hall, Long Acre, on 6 April 1854, and, most recently, on 23 March 1858 (Bennett, *Life*, 203–8, 232–5, 276–9). Henry Leslie's choir was formed in 1855, introducing strict discipline learned from German choirs, and gave its first performance at the Hanover Square Rooms on 22 May 1856, first singing unaccompanied madrigals and partsongs with

Footnote 3 continues on page 34

5. John Hullah conducting at the opening of St. Martin's Hall, London, 1850
An example of the large orchestral and choral forces mentioned by Bennett, showing also the tendency of English audiences to treat concerts as social events.

I have already said that the supply of amateur aid seems ever equal to the demand. One circumstance to this effect is within my own experience. <Last year> {The year before last},[1] a large society which had usually given its valuable help to the annual performance <for the benefit> of a very important musical society, suddenly withdrew its aid <from some peculiar reasons, known only to themselves>, and the places of five hundred seceding vocal performers had to be immediately filled up. This was done in a few days with little more than ordinary exertion, and as I was the appointed conductor, it gave me extreme pleasure and surprise to find that this quickly collected body formed the finest chorus I had ever heard.[2]

In my anxiety to do justice to the promoters and supporters of the large choral societies, let me not neglect the societies specially formed for the production of instrumental music. These societies in the bulk are less indebted to amateur assistance than are the choral societies. Still, however, speaking firstly of our Philharmonic Society (now in its forty sixth season), its very existence is traceable to an amateur spirit. At its birth and long afterwards, our most eminent pianists & composers (John Cramer, Griffin, Potter, & other celebrities) became amateurs in the orchestra and took up orchestral instruments to set the institution safely afloat.[3]

about sixty singers, but gradually increasing the numbers so that larger works could be undertaken (Silantien, 'Part-song', 150–61). The Vocal Association was also founded in 1855 on the lines of a German *Gesangverein*, with Julius Benedict as conductor, and gave its first series of concerts at the Crystal Palace, Sydenham, the following year (Musgrave, *Crystal Palace*, 27–47). The London Polyhymnian Choir for male voices, modelled on the Cologne Choral Union, was established in 1856 by William Rea, a pupil of Bennett's; it had reached 100 voices by the 1859 season, when it gave three concerts at the Hanover Square Rooms (*Musical World* 37 (1859), 595–6). John Hullah's sight-singing classes, begun in 1841, operated in St. Martin's Hall from its opening in 1850 until its destruction by fire in 1863, and he gave public concerts there from time to time (see Plate 5).

1 This change must have been made when the lecture was repeated at Sheffield in 1859.

2 See Bennett, *Life*, 257. A fuller account emerges from the minute books of the Royal Society of Musicians. The society was planning its annual performance of *Messiah* for May 1857 under the direction of Michael Costa as usual. On 12 April word was received that Costa would not conduct unless his own list of soloists was accepted. After a failed attempt at compromise Costa withdrew (taking with him the choir of the Sacred Harmonic Society), Bennett was asked to take his place, and the concert was postponed to 3 June. Between 3 and 8 May the conductors of several choirs were successfully approached to provide singers, and a choral rehearsal was fixed for 25 May.

3 Johann Baptist Cramer and George Eugene Griffin, both prominent solo pianists, were founding members of the Philharmonic Society. It is true that in the early, idealistic years of the society, many leading soloists would play their part in the orchestra in democratic fashion, but as pianists Cramer and Griffin were not in a position to do so. Cramer took turns with Clementi in the task of directing several concerts from the piano. Cipriani

Nor must I forget to mention the strong body of instrumental amateurs formed under the title of 'The Amateur Musical Society', giving their concerts at the Hanover Rooms, [or] the amateur instrumentalists practising under the guidance of my friend Mr Dando at Crosby Hall, to whose zeal and activity in the cause of music the City of London must feel deeply indebted.[1]

However, in passing from the consideration of purely choral societies to <instrumental societies> {those combining instrumental music [with choral]},[2] there is no doubt that we have more to do with professors than with amateurs.

There is another class of musical entertainment within the metropolis which receives an enormous amount of public patronage: I allude to the 'Italian opera'. Of late years it seems to have been necessary to employ two theatres and two companies to provide for the wants of those who delight in this species of music.[3] I wish I could with any conscience acknowledge that the art in the present day is much indebted to the Italian operas for its onward progress in this country, but as far as music composition is concerned, I believe the reverse to be the case.

I give you the opinion of an eminent musical historian upon this subject:

> The present Italian composers are mere imitators of Rossini: and are much more successful in copying his defects than his beauties. They are, like him, full of mannerism; with this difference, that his manner was his own, while theirs is his. They occasionally produce pretty melodies, a faculty possessed, to some extent, by every Italian composer, however low his grade; but in general, their airs are strings of commonplace passages borrowed chiefly from Rossini, and employed without regard to the

Potter, who was to be Bennett's principal teacher, appeared frequently as a piano soloist in the Philharmonic concerts, beginning in 1816. See Ehrlich, *First Philharmonic*.

1 The Amateur Musical Society was founded in 1847 for private musical enjoyment by a predominantly aristocratic membership. It soon began to give concerts, first for invited guests and then for the public (Temperley, 'Instrumental Music', 73). In an unconnected initiative, Joseph Dando (1806–94), a leading violinist, leased and restored Crosby Hall, Bishopsgate Street, in 1842 and used it both for professional subscription concerts of chamber music and for many amateur activities. See Scholes, *Mirror*, 205–6.

2 This change may also have been made for Sheffield. Below, on the same page, is a portion covered by a piece of blank paper pasted over. It contains a pencilled note: 'a regret that after all choral music is too much regarded to the neglect of instrumental music', and, in ink, a sentence about choral festivals that was later incorporated into the main text.

3 The Royal Italian Opera at Covent Garden was founded in 1847, while Her Majesty's Theatre continued its annual opera seasons dating from the early eighteenth century. Rivalry was intense; the manager of Her Majesty's, Benjamin Lumley, had to close the company after the 1852 season due to financial difficulties, but it reopened in 1856 after a fire at Covent Garden.

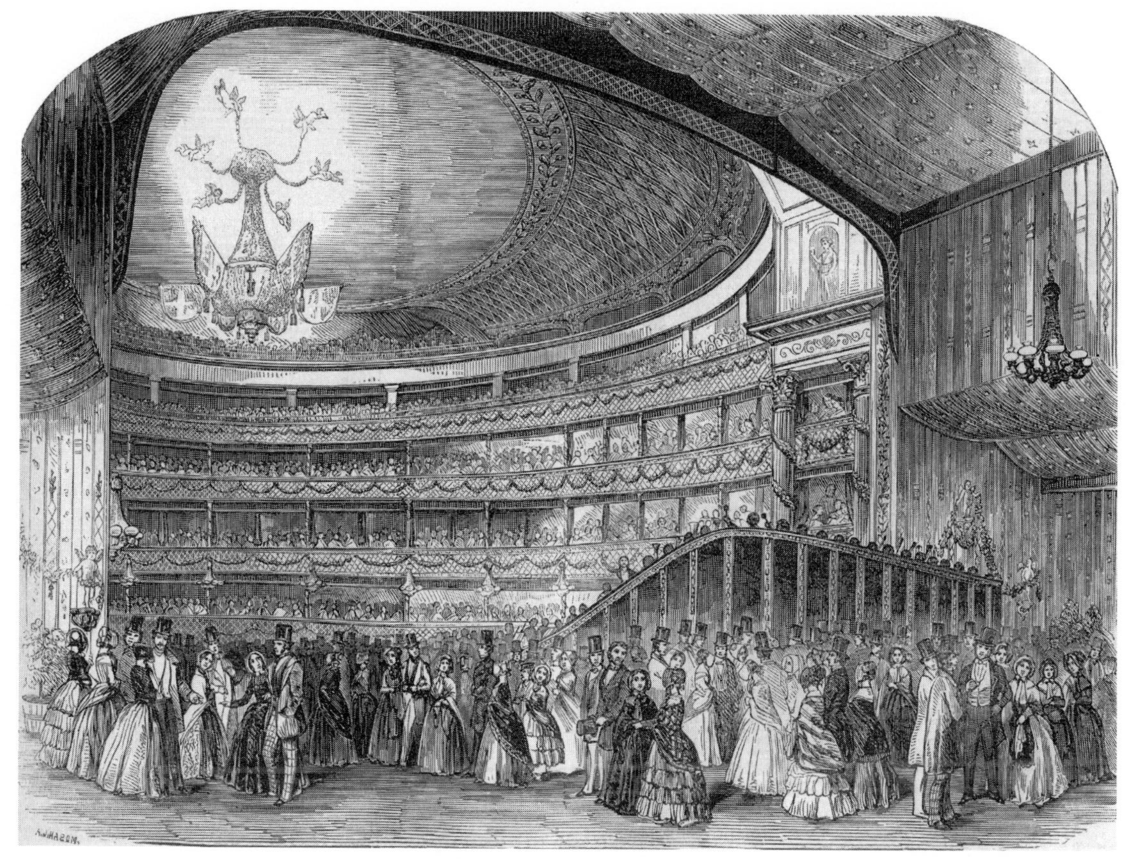

6. Jullien's Promenade Concerts at Drury Lane Theatre, 1847

Promenade concerts offered opportunities for the less affluent to attend great musical events, but they evidently used them for display of fashionable clothes rather than for serious contemplation of music.

> sentiment and expression required by the scene. Their concerted pieces are clumsy and inartificial; and their loud and boisterous accompaniments show a total ignorance of orchestral composition. This general description applies to them all.[1]

When, presently, I shall make an enquiry as to 'home music', I shall be obliged to point to the flimsy arrangements of modern Italian operas as one of the causes which militate against pure and classical taste in this country.

But to be just, as I trust to be found, the Italian operas have given a powerful impetus to performance. Nobody can deny to the Italians the gift of singing, and singing according to nature; and the long succession of Italian vocalists visiting this country has no doubt stimulated our native artists to achieve that reputation which they now enjoy. The orchestral portion at these dramatic performances deserves also the warmest acknowledgement. It is much to the credit of England that no orchestra in any theatre in Europe can surpass that of Covent Garden.[2]

Turning our thoughts to the provinces, we are reminded of those astounding musical gatherings so fitly denominated 'Festivals', which at one grasp call every kind of society & all species of performance into one bond of union.

The greatest[3] of these festivals, that of Birmingham, which takes place triennially, as do most of the provincial festivals, must cause intense wonder and delight to those who for the first time take part either as performer or listener. Even to the experienced London musician, who has probably played or heard every note before, which is provided for him at Birmingham, there is a freshness in the scene, and a charm in the excitement, which cannot fail to arouse his enthusiasm.

This Birmingham [Festival], as many of my hearers may be aware, was the scene of that last great triumph of the illustrious Mendelssohn, when he produced his 'Elijah'![4]

At these great meetings every class of music is provided. To the morning performances you are attracted by the 'sublime oratorio', in the evening a philharmonic concert awaits your patronage. The symphony, the overture, the concerto, the Italian & English schools, [all] are fairly represented, and the performance gives delight to an audience which in about four days has subscribed something like twelve or fourteen

1 Quoted from Hogarth, *Musical History*, 398.

2 Here Bennett inserted a note to himself: 'Allude to the ready preparation of Meyerbeer operas'.

3 Bennett later changed 'greatest' to 'longest established', probably when revising the lecture for use in Sheffield. In fact, however, the Three Choirs Festival was older.

4 Mendelssohn conducted the premiere performance of *Elijah* at the Birmingham Festival on 26 August 1846.

thousand pounds to meet the expenses. Long may these musical gatherings flourish, alike honourable to England, and beneficial to art! It is gratifying to know that they are even on the increase. Leeds will shortly compete with other large towns in the matter of music festivals. In the present year it is intended to open the magnificent new town hall, for which an organ has been built at the cost of about £4000.[1]

I wish that the plan of my lecture would have allowed me to say all the severe part at first and leave the pleasant portion for a conclusion, but to speak candidly, all the complimentary part is finished, and it is my duty now to put the question 'What is done for music at home?' And I much fear the enquiry will terminate unsatisfactorily. Nevertheless it will be my duty before I close to tender my humble advice in the matter, and I feel assured that however plainly I may speak upon the subject, the sincerity of my feelings will be duly allowed by an audience so unaccustomed to any thing but the real truth in art and science.

<In addition to the smaller pieces which may always be culled from large works,>[2] there is a great quantity of music, the creation of the great masters, which from its exquisite delicacy and minuteness of construction is termed chamber music as distinguished from that composed for the concert room. All the great masters have contributed to this class. In such a collection you will find the harpsichord lessons of Bach, Scarlatti, and Handel, the vocal chamber duets of Handel, the charming canzonets of Haydn, the beautiful pianoforte music of Mozart with and without accompaniments,[3] not including his concertos, which are designed for the concert room. The pianoforte music of Clementi & Dussek, many highly elaborated miniature pieces of the masterly Hummel, the enchanting pianoforte songs and duets of Mendelssohn,[4] {the graceful vocal music of Bishop, Attwood, Horsley, & others}[5] and above all the

[1] The last two sentences were later replaced by the following: 'Yorkshire has now competed with the other great districts, Bradford & Leeds having already taken their permanent stand in the matter of these large festivals.' This is written in Mary Bennett's hand. Below it is a pencilled note in Bennett's hand: 'Leeds/In our own county'. These changes were no doubt made for Sheffield. The first Bradford choral festival was given in August 1853 in the newly built St. George's Hall, while the Leeds Festival was to open under Bennett's direction in the new Town Hall on 8 September 1858, with a performance of *Elijah*.

[2] This phrase deleted, and replaced by the following (in Mary Bennett's hand): 'In advising you as to the course you should take in improving your taste & cultivating your family concert, I must draw your attention to the fact that in addition to the smaller pieces which may always be culled from large works, . . .'

[3] By 'pianoforte music . . . with . . . accompaniments' Bennett was using the older term for violin and piano sonatas, piano trios, and the like.

[4] That is, songs and vocal duets with pianoforte accompaniment.

[5] Bennett later added Barnett and Smart to this list of English composers of vocal music. (Full names and dates of all persons mentioned are provided in the index.)

rich store of music written for bowed instruments such as the trios of Handel and Corelli, the quartets {&c} of Haydn, Mozart, {Beethoven}, Spohr, Mendelssohn, & others.

All this music which I have mentioned is in its right place in the drawing room of a private house, and although much of it is heard elsewhere, and its introduction in concert rooms [is] highly creditable to those professors who are determined that these comparatively neglected gems shall be heard in one place or other,[1] still its effect is impaired by removal from that sphere for which it was composed.

Now having gone through a catalogue of chamber music, may I ask if such music is often to [be] found in 'English private society' <in a population of two million>?[2]

Will the love and appreciation of music, as exemplified in the performances we meet with in private houses, bear any comparison to that zeal and enthusiasm bestowed upon public music, and to which I have testified in the early part of my lecture? Can one believe that the immense out-of-door excitement in the course of the art, produces so few musical homes? Whence should musical cultivation emanate, should it not be from home? How many houses should I have to visit before I found any family earnestly engaged in the practice of good concerted music? Should I not rather be certain to find specimens of that hateful form of composition, fantasias from modern Italian operas, on the pianoforte desk? I will quote a few words from the clever Mr Fétis upon the modern pianoforte fantasias, in which I must entirely concur:

> A certain frivolity of taste, which has invaded music, has substituted, in the place of the serious forms of pieces, a lighter sort of composition called fantasia. The fantasia was originally a piece in which the composer abandoned himself to all the impulses of his imagination. The inspiration of the moment, art & even science (tho' carefully concealed) constituted the fantasia, as Bach, Handel, and Mozart made it. But this is not what we now understand by that word. In no composition can there be less of fantasy than in those of the present day which bear that name. To hear one modern fantasia is to hear the whole. They are all made upon one model.

1 Originally this passage read: 'and although much of it is heard elsewhere, and its introduction is highly creditable to those professors who are determined to present these comparatively neglected gems to their friends in concert rooms, still its effect is impaired . . .' Regular public concerts devoted to chamber music were initiated in 1835, one of the pioneers being Joseph Dando: see Temperley, 'Instrumental Music', i.94–7; by the time Bennett was speaking, they were securely established in Ella's *Musical Union* (Bashford, 'John Ella') and other series.

2 The bracketed phrase, later deleted for the Sheffield lectures, refers to London, whose population was reported at approximately 2.3 million in the 1851 census.

> The theme even is not original, since it almost always consists of the melody of a romance, or an air of an opera.[1]

Now although in the words of Sir Joshua Reynolds, 'It is the lowest style of art, whether of poetry, painting, or music, which can be said in the vulgar sense to be naturally pleasing',[2] does it therefore follow that high class music is necessarily sombre or should under any circumstances be dreary? The examples which I shall offer you this evening will I hope relieve you of any fear you may have on this score. Cannot Mozart and Haydn be joyous and ever classical? Has not Beethoven represented to the life the dance of the happy villagers in his 'Pastorale Symphony', and what work can surpass this in masterly construction and treatment? Are not Weber and Mendelssohn classical composers, and can even the uneducated person listen unmoved to the unearthly strains of 'Oberon' and the bewitching themes of the 'Midsummer Night's Dream'?[3]

Now apart from the catalogue of pure chamber music which a few minutes since I brought to your notice, there exists a large amount of concert music so beautifully arranged for home performance that I cannot but recommend its adoption, as a means to elevate and maintain style in musical feeling and performance. Of such are the symphonies of Mozart and Beethoven arranged by the great Hummel, [and] the overtures & symphonies of Mendelssohn, in all cases, I believe, arranged by himself; and let me remark that short of an orchestra there can be nothing more effective or more likely to do justice to the instrumental works of the great masters than a good arrangement for two performers on the pianoforte.

With all my complaints I do not despond. All things considered there is perhaps only one country in Europe whose musical reputation and chances I would exchange for our own. This is musical Germany. Who can deny to the Germans the merits of having brought music to its present perfection, after the Italians had so suffered it to decline? I need not take up your time in insisting upon the vast debt of gratitude due to that country which has so long supplied us with rich music. Whether Germany at this precise moment is quite what it was, I must not now enquire. That will belong to my fourth lecture, but I am anxious to draw your attention to two points wherein we are greatly the losers, and the

[1] Quoted from Fétis, *History of Music*, 17, but with considerable omissions. See also Yang, 'Bennett's Fantasia'.

[2] Quoted (perhaps from memory) from Reynolds, *Discourses*, 226: 'It is the lowest style only of arts, whether of painting, poetry, or music, that may be said, in the vulgar sense, to be naturally pleasing.'

[3] Here, Bennett began a sentence 'In the "Creation" of Haydn, although', then deleted it.

7. *Hausmusik* in the home of the Gutzwiller family, Basel, 1849

From an oil painting. Though in Switzerland, it well illustrates Bennett's description of serious Germanic music-making as part of family life, where those who are not taking part continue their work (or play) as they listen.

Germans greatly the gainers, and as I speak from experience I can speak upon the matter with confidence.

The first point is, that German homes are musical – good music and good performance is the rule in Germany, in England it is the exception. The Germans do not wait for periodical concerts for their food; they find it in their own resources. They enjoy music for itself and apart from display. How many delightful hours have I spent in German families, and witnessed the unaffected performance of some choice gems, ever at hand!

Now take up the music books in English drawing rooms, and what a strange jumble you find <and how many young ladies would you find ready and willing to perform the office of accompanyist?> Sentimental ballads, with words and music alike common place, but with very highly embellished title pages – hashes from the Trovatore[1] – Ethiopian melodies, which being first introduced as caricatures are now accepted as

[1] Bennett has a point here. The British Library holds at least 83 distinct fantasias, pot-pourris and similar pieces based on themes from Verdi's *Il Trovatore* (1853),

8. 'Music in the Drawing-Room', 1849

Designed to illustrate a satirical account of music at social gatherings in fashionable English society. The artist has contrived to suggest a somewhat frivolous and amateurish approach to music-making.

genuine music and performed with all proper solemnity[1] – ornamented psalm tunes, or psalm tunes with variations[2] – but I need only refer you to the supplement of the Times[3] to show you the style of music which unfortunately now prevails in private society.[4] It is all this which brings a taint upon this branch of the fine arts and causes it to be looked upon as a light and frivolous accomplishment.

The second point in which England suffers in comparison with

published in or before the year in which Bennett spoke these words (1858). See Balchin, *CPM*, 58:137–40.

1 Songs from minstrel shows, imported from the United States and then imitated in Britain, in which white performers in blackface impersonated negroes. See Scott, 'Blackface Minstrels'.

2 We have failed to locate any published examples of psalm-tune variations for piano from this period.

3 Presumably Bennett is referring to the monthly supplements published with the *Musical Times*, although these consisted largely of anthems and partsongs.

4 Bennett first wrote: '. . . which, unfortunately prevalent in private houses, now prevails'.

Germany is the excitement seemingly inseparable from concerts and other performances. Notwithstanding the almost numberless concerts now given in London, to go to a concert is still an event. No concert which begins before eight o'clock in the evening is considered fashionable, and any programme which would come to an end before eleven or twelve would be considered meagre. Many an English household even dreads the name of a concert, which upsets all domestic arrangements long beforehand, and prevents anything like tranquility long afterwards. <Firstly the dinner hour must be altered, and the patient head of the family circle hurried off after all the day's fatigue of his private avocations.> So it is that a large portion of the English public are deterred from giving in their adhesion to music, simply because they never hear of it except as connected with hot rooms and late hours.

How is it in Germany? I will give you a faithful answer to this question. Music never interferes with the ordinary avocations of a German. 'It is never in the way, and never out of the way.'[1] Will you believe me when I tell you that after having enjoyed an entire performance of the opera at the Leipzig theatre, I have seen the doors locked at half past eight in the evening, and that the grand concerts of that town have decided the fate of many a composer and performer long before supper time – nine o'clock?

Why should those who are willing to know music and to love it be forced only to acknowledge its claims by entering under large porticoes, and seating themselves in large halls? Are there no means by which the sensitive person or the invalid can be introduced to the choicest treasures of musical art? Is music only to be heard when the sun has gone down? Why not make it a kind of daily bread in our houses: the portfolios of good music ever at hand; the young people admonished, that to trifle with music is to trifle with one of the greatest gifts which our creator has bestowed upon us, a gift which is destined to sing his praises 'upon the lute and harp in the cymbals and dances'.[2] Let the young men choose those instruments which will bring them into contact with the works of the great masters, and avoid those instruments more fitted for the open air than the quiet of an English drawing room, and for which nothing but light and frivolous music is written.[3]

Whilst public entertainments are increasing their dimensions and importance, let each family circle be working for the art at home. Let music be loved for its own sake, and not estimated according to the

1 This sentence is in quotation marks, but its origin has not been traced.

2 A reference to Psalm 150.

3 Bennett is referring, no doubt, to instruments associated with street music: the concertina, accordion, banjo, hurdy-gurdy, tin whistle, mandoline, zither, and possibly guitar (see Crowest, *Phases of Musical England*, 112–41).

applause which it brings to the performer. Let the family concert performance include such specimens as those I am now about to submit to you, and of which there is such an abundance.

Let the names of the great masters so frequently mentioned by me this evening become as 'household words', and then will the art prosper without limit in this country.

That England has the power to become a really 'musical nation' no one can deny. That it is at present fully deserving that title I dare not venture to affirm.

<I have arranged my illustration of this lecture into the form of a little concert, which with your permission we will now commence. In my capacity of lecturer therefore I respectfully take my leave for this occasion, thanking you very much for the kind attention which you have paid to my remarks.>

PROGRAMME[1]

Grand Duett in A flat [for four hands, Op. 92], 1st movement	Hummel
Trio, 'Soave sia il vento' [from *Così fan tutte*]	Mozart
Canzonet, 'The Mermaid' [from *VI Original Canzonettas*, i]	Haydn
Sonata, violin and pianoforte, in G major [Op. 30, No. 3; or Op. 96]	Beethoven
Duett, 'Come be gay' ['Schelm! halt fest', from *Der Freischütz*]	Weber
Song, 'The Savoyard' ['Pagenlied' from *2 Gesänge, Eichendorff* (1835)]	Mendelssohn
Song, 'I am a roamer' ['Ich bin ein vielgereister Mann', from *Die Heimkehr aus dem Fremde* ('Son and Stranger', Op. 89)]	Mendelssohn
Two-part songs, 'Greeting', 'The May Bells' ['Gruss', 'Maiglockchen', Op. 63, Nos. 3, 6]	Mendelssohn
Glee, 'The Loadstars' [for two sopranos and bass (1797)]	Shield

1 For the programme of the quite different concert presented at this point when the lecture was repeated at Sheffield, with programme notes, see Appendix 1.

2

On the Visits of Illustrious Foreign Musicians to England

London Institution, 15 April 1858
Sheffield Literary and Philosophical Society, 29 April 1859

When foreign writers upon music make up their minds to do justice to England, then will it be universally acknowledged that this country has performed a most important share in connection with the progress of the art. Symptoms of an improved and more liberal state of things on the part of foreign critics are indeed now apparent, but until recently one could not but be amused at the ingenuity with which our Continental musical censors,[1] when speaking of the great composers of Europe, avoided nearly all allusion to England, <which had been the first to appreciate them and their works, in many cases the country of their adoption, and where they found their talents most appreciated and most rewarded> – {the country which has ever been the most ready to welcome, to appreciate, and to reward the sons of art}.

In collecting my material for this evening's lecture, <I was even unprepared for the intimate connexion there has so long been, between this country and foreign musicians, and considering myself fully armed to defend my position, I really found that I had underestimated my strength.> I was reminded that I had forgotten to include one great name in my enumeration of those who had delighted to visit England, in a time that England, by means of the little facility of travelling, might be said to be almost inaccessible.[2]

Let me give you a complete list of those great heroes of the musical art

1 'Continental musical censors': corrections show that this phrase had two earlier forms, 'Continental neighbours' and 'Continental musical critics'.

2 This means that until Bennett started serious work on the subject he had overlooked an important visitor to England. A deleted passage later in the text shows that the name was that of Gluck.

who have honoured England with their love, and whom England has delighted to honour: Handel, Gluck, Mozart, Haydn, Clementi, Dussek, Spohr, Rossini, Weber, Hummel, Mendelssohn. Here is a long string of names, known to past England and present England, names of illustrious musicians – all of whom had no reason to regret their visits to us.

It is not my intention this evening to entertain you with much of the personal histories of these great men, nor indeed to enter more fully into their artistical career than will just serve to connect one epoch with another and maintain the plan of my lecture. How willingly would I spend hours, could time afford it, in going into the history, public & private, of any one of the names I have mentioned, but on this occasion having only time to take a cursory view of art and artists as connected with England from Handel to Mendelssohn, I must refrain from any such attempt.

To those who are anxious and willing to make themselves acquainted with the personal and artistic lives of the great musicians with whom we shall have to deal this evening, I shall beg leave to recommend that they consult many works from which I myself shall freely quote. Such are the works of Burney & Hawkins; the Musical Biography of Hogarth; the very interesting and beautiful work, 'The Life of Mozart' from the pen of Mr Edward Holmes, a work [which] whilst only professing to give the life of Mozart includes many important facts and data connected with that epoch; the life of Handel by Schloecher; the new life of the same great man by Dr Chrysander.[1]

Handel

Handel arrived in England in 1710, a young man of five [and] twenty. He had by that time acquired a great reputation as a composer of Italian operas, and it was in that capacity that he began his career in this country.

He was first applied to by Aaron Hill, a celebrated but now forgotten tragic poet of that day, who was then manager of the Haymarket Theatre, to compose an opera which was entitled 'Rinaldo', which it was said was composed in a fortnight. The subject, taken from Tasso, was sketched by Hill himself.[2]

The great foreign artist did not find England a bed of roses on his first arrival. Addison, who knew as little of Italian poetry as of music of any

1 For full citations of these works see the Bibliography.

2 Giacomo Rossi's libretto was based on a scenario by Hill after Tasso's *Gerusalemme liberata*.

kind, sneered at this work in one of the early numbers of the Spectator,[1] but notwithstanding his hostility, and that of several of his literary brethren, 'Rinaldo' was highly successful & established Handel's fame as an operatic writer.

In the year 1718, Handel undertook the direction of the music at the Chapel of the Duke of Chandos at Cannons, near Edgware. While there he composed the Chandos Anthems, the music to Gay's charming pastoral 'Acis & Galatea', & the oratorio of 'Esther,' the herald of a series of gigantic conceptions which will ever associate the name of Handel with England, his adopted country.

To the worshippers of Handel, in this country numberless, I would recommend a pilgrimage to Whitchurch, Little Stanmore, where stands the original private chapel of the Duke of Chandos (Handel's munificent patron), now a parish church, where is still to be found the identical organ, at which Handel constantly presided <– a hallowed spot>.[2]

It was not until long after this period that Handel really commenced his career as an immortal composer of oratorios. He continued to be immersed in the turmoils and difficulty of the Italian opera. For many years he was manager of the theatre in the Haymarket for which he composed a series of beautiful works.

At length, having given offence to a party of the aristocracy, a combination was formed against him, and a rival house established in Lincoln's Inn Fields – much like the double Italian opera of the present day. For this rival establishment the then celebrated Bononcini was engaged as composer, and although so far inferior to Handel proved for a time a formidable competitor.[3]

The whole musical world of that day entered into warfare upon the subject, and so violent was the feud that even personal friendships were sacrificed.

To Handel the result of the struggle was ruinous. His life at this period presents nothing but an arduous & calamitous contest with the difficulties which surrounded him; he finally abandoned the Italian opera. But when will the name Handel be forgotten? And who now knows anything about the once-famed Bononcini?

I will now present you with two specimens from the works of Handel: the one, an instrumental trio;[4] the other, a song from the Italian opera of

1 Joseph Addison's scathing critique of *Rinaldo* in the *Spectator*, No. 5 (6 March 1711), actually has little to say about the music.

2 St. Lawrence, Whitchurch, with organ by Abraham Jordan.

3 In fact Bononcini was not involved in the rivalry between the two companies, which lasted from 1733 to 1738, but he had competed with Handel in the London opera scene of the 1720s.

4 This is deleted, here and in the listing just below, and replaced by 'the Overture to

'Sosarme' which is better known under the title of 'Lord, Remember David.'

Trio — violin, alto, & cello[1]	Handel
Air — 'Rendi il sereno' (Lord, remember David)[2]	Handel

These are beautiful examples of the art as it then stood. Still there was a certain stiffness of manner in the construction both of the vocal and instrumental music of this period that seemed to require reform.

[**Gluck**]

In their respective branches, the great reformers were Gluck and Haydn. <I had omitted the name of Gluck in my syllabus, because he had not presented himself to my mind.>

Gluck was born [in] 1714. He (Gluck) came to England [in] 1745, then 30 years old. He was engaged to write two operas, one of which, 'The Fall of the Giants', was intended as a compliment to the Duke of Cumberland, the victor of Culloden, the giants who fell being the unfortunate adherents of the Stuart race.[3]

Burney mentions the following conversation in speaking of Gluck:[4]

> He told me that he owed entirely to England the study of nature in his dramatic compositions: he went thither at a very disadvantageous period; Handel was then so high in fame that no one would willingly listen to any other than to his compositions.
>
> The rebellion broke out, all foreigners were regarded as dangerous to the state; the opera-house was shut up, by the order of the Lord Chamberlain and it was with great difficulty and address that Lord Middlesex obtained permission to open it again with a temporary & political

Esther', which does not agree with the printed programme for either London or Sheffield. For the musical examples used at Sheffield, see Appendix.

[1] 'Alto' means viola. No such work by Handel exists; this must have been an arrangement.

[2] This adaptation of the aria 'Rendi'l sereno al ciglio', from Handel's *Sosarme*, was made by Samuel Arnold as part of his pastiche oratorio *Redemption* (1786) and became enormously popular in that form.

[3] The Duke of Cumberland, a son of George II, commanded the royal army that defeated the Jacobite Rebellion, led by Prince Charles Edward Stuart, at the battle of Culloden on 16 April 1746. Gluck's opera, *La caduta de' giganti*, was actually performed before that battle, on 7 January 1746.

[4] The long quotation from Burney's *Present State of Music in Germany* (pp. 263–4), and the paragraph following it, are in Mary Bennett's hand, and were presumably added for Sheffield in order to provide an adequate treatment of Gluck's visit to England. The quotation follows Burney exactly except for punctuation and paragraph structure.

> performance, La Caduta de Giganti (The Fall of the Giants). This Gluck worked upon with fear and trembling not only on account of the few friends he had in England, but from an apprehension of riot and popular fury, at the opening of the theatre, in which none but foreigners and papists were employed. He then studied the English taste; remarked particularly what the audience seemed most to feel, and finding that plainness and simplicity had the greatest effect upon them, he has ever since that time endeavoured to write for the voice more in the natural tones of the human affections and passions, than to flatter the lovers of deep science or difficult execution, and it may be remarked that most of his airs in Orfeo are as plain and simple as English ballads.

But though M. Gluck studies simple nature so much in his cantilena or voice part, yet in his accompaniments he is not only often learned but elaborate; and in this particular, he is even more than a poet and musician, he is an excellent painter: his instruments frequently delineated the situation of the actor, and gave a high colouring to passion.

Handel pronounced this work {The Fall of the Giants} detestable, but notwithstanding this high authority against him, Gluck was one of the great men who established an era in the art, being founder of the great school of dramatic music. Rousseau was enthusiastic in his love for this composer. 'We know', he says, 'how far removed are these pure melodic forms, so well accented, and strongly impressed with fine dramatic genius, from the convulsive system of the present day <the only object of which seems to [be to] animate the convivial party and assist digestion>.'

I now beg to introduce a song of Gluck from his opera of 'Orpheus' entitled 'Che faro senza Eurydice', which is not included in my syllabus, but which as a specimen is a most valuable link between Handel & Mozart.

Air — 'Che faro senza Eurydice' (from Orfeo ed Euridice)	Gluck

Mozart[1]

In the history of music we should naturally place Mozart after Haydn, but in my plan of this evening Mozart must come before Haydn, his visit to England being much the earlier of the two. The <Mozart> family <consisting of himself, father, & sister> set out for England by way of Calais in 1764, and remained here until the end of the following year lodging in Frith Street, Soho. The two children played to their Majesties on the 27 of April & again in the month of May, when the boy played on

1 Apart from the heading and one correction, the whole section on Mozart except the last paragraph ('Before leaving Mozart . . .') is in Mary Bennett's hand.

the King's organ with as much success as at Versailles. During his residence here he composed six sonatas which were published and dedicated to the Queen, he being then only eight years old. On the 27 of May he made his first appearance at the English court, an appearance as honourable to his august patrons as to himself. His father in a letter to his wife says:

> What we have here experienced surpasses everything, we could not believe ourselves in the presence of their Majesties, a week afterwards we were walking in St. James's Park when the King & Queen came driving by, and altho' we were all differently dressed, they knew & saluted us[;] the King in particular threw open the carriage window[,] put out his head[,] and laughingly greeted us with head and hands, particularly our Master Wolfgang. On the 19th of May we were again with their Majesties from 6 to ten. Nobody was present but the two princes, the brother of the King & the brother of the Queen.
>
> We shall do well enough (speaking of pecuniary matters) if thro' God's blessing we all keep well and particularly our intrepid Wolfgang.
>
> The King <George 3rd> placed before him <the boy> pieces by Wagenseil, [Johann Christian] Bach, Abel, and Handel, all of which he played off.
>
> He played on the King's organ in such a manner, that his hearers preferred him on the organ to the clavier, he then accompanied the Queen in an air and a performer on the Flauto Traverso in a solo, at last he took up the bass part of one of Handel's airs, and upon the mere bass performed a most beautiful melody that astonished everybody.[1]

The concert of the family on the 5th of June was most fashionably patronised and very profitable; the father was alarmed at the extraordinary expense of an English orchestra. He records with due honour to the musical profession that most of the musicians would take nothing. A concert being given at Ranelagh [Gardens] for a charity, the father says: 'I have permitted Wolfgang to play the British patriot and perform an organ concerto on this occasion. Observe, this is the way to gain the love of the English.'[2]

Towards the close of 1764 appeared a third set of sonatas,[3] dedicated to Queen Charlotte, for which she sent 50 guineas. Young as he was he even at this time exercised a permanent influence on English music. The first introduction of clavier duets (pieces for 4 hands) is ascribed to him. Among the trophies of his achievements in England, the father preserved

1 This seems to be adapted from Holmes, *Mozart*, 32–3, with several omissions and a few insignificant changes. Holmes in turn left out much of the original letter.

2 Holmes, 33. The organ concerto was an invention of Handel's, and at this date existed only in England.

3 K. 10–15.

an official letter from the British Museum, acknowledging an anthem and other M. S. compositions[,] the performances of his 'very ingenious son.'[1] However, as time wore on, the novelty declined, and Mozart's father becoming dissatisfied left England Sept. 1765.

There seems good authority for stating that in later life Mozart entertained a wish to settle in England, but this we know was never carried out.

As a specimen of Mozart's early operatic writing, we will present you with an exquisite song from the Seraglio.[2]

Air — 'Wer ein Liebchen' — (Die Entführung)	Mozart

Before leaving Mozart, I am anxious to grasp at every minute circumstance which connects him with us. I again quote from Holmes' Life. His father having caught a severe cold in London, every instrument was obliged to be mute. The boy in order to employ himself, wrote a symphony[3] which was the first attempt of that kind. His sister sat near him, copying while he was at work, and he said to her 'remind me that I give the horns something good to do.'

<With regard to the sonata of which we will now play a portion, it is said Mozart played it with a female violin player at her concert, without having written a note of his own part, and without any kind of rehearsal.>

Duett [i.e. sonata for violin and piano], B flat	Mozart

Haydn

Haydn, the author of 118 symphonies & 82 quartets, the great musical reformer to whom the art is so deeply indebted, was born in the year 1732.

His first visit to England was in 1790,[4] when he came by invitation of Salomon to conduct and compose pieces for a set of concerts. He remained in London twelve months, during which time he produced his twelve grand symphonies and his beautiful canzonets, written to English words, with a host of other works.

1 The anthem 'God is our refuge' and the previously mentioned sonatas (K. 10–15).

2 Revised for Sheffield: 'As a specimen of Mozart's early operatic writing I could refer you to many exquisite songs from the Seraglio but I will myself play you one of his earliest and [one of his] later sonatas for the pianoforte.'

3 K. 16, or possibly an earlier work now lost. See Zaslaw, *Mozart's Symphonies*, 16–20.

4 In fact Haydn arrived in England on 1 January 1791.

It is interesting to know that there are still those living who remember the visits of this great man, and who can testify to the warmth in which he was welcomed by the English public, and the influence which his presence and example had upon the profession.[1] Haydn also on his part confesses to great gain, in becoming first acquainted with the music of Handel, and also having the opportunity of being present at the Concerts of Ancient Music, which were at that time splendidly patronised and supported by rich talent.

This testimony of Haydn is valuable to England as pointing very distinctly to the healthy state of musical appreciation at that period, and which has gradually developed itself up to the present moment. In addition to his symphonies, ——————————,[2] one can readily fancy the delight and rapture with which his quartets were received, that new form of composition, so much in advance of that in vogue in the time of Handel.[3]

I will now introduce one of the charming English canzonets written to the words of Mrs Hunter, and which for grace & tenderness are unequalled – <& a song from The Seasons, on a theme connected with the symphonies written for Salomon.>

Canzonet — 'The Season Comes'[4]	Haydn
Air — 'With joy the impatient Husbandman'[5]	Haydn

Hummel

was born in 1780, [and] came to England as a boy in the years 1791 & 1792. Had it not been for this fact, I should have placed him as in my syllabus, after Weber, for it was only at a later time that his visit exercised any influence upon art.[6] As a pianist & composer for his instrument, he was warmly received and appreciated in this country. His elegant and refined style has been the model for many a distinguished musician and performer.

1 One of these was Sir George Smart. See below, p. 118.

2 Bennett here drew a long line.

3 Here Bennett added the following notes: 'Dr Callcott in his diary for 1791 says (Jany 31) I saw Haydn for the first time [to]day and walked with him and Salomon / Hon. Degree to Haydn at Oxford – July 8 1791 Vice Chancellor Dr Chapman'.

4 'Recollection' from *VI English Canzonetts*, Book I (1794).

5 From *The Seasons* (1801). Haydn humorously depicts the ploughman whistling and singing the tune of the second movement of Symphony No. 94 (the 'Surprise').

6 Hummel paid three late visits to England in 1830, 1831 and 1833.

Hummel is also an excellent composer of church music, the only drawback to his reputation being the want of originality <in his works>.

Whilst speaking of Hummel in connection with the pianoforte, I take the opportunity of recognising the claims of many other great foreign masters, who like him laboured in the right direction. Such were Clementi, Dussek, Woelfl, Steibelt, Ries, to all of whom and many others, we owe our thanks that pianoforte playing in this country has attained its present perfection.[1]

Mr O'Leary will now perform two studies by Hummel, very characteristic of that composer's style.

Pianoforte Studies[2]	Hummel

Spohr

The next illustrious visitor to this country, and one happily still living to the delight of his friends and the benefit of art, is Louis Spohr. This musician came by invitation of the Philharmonic Society in the year 1819,[3] and performed in a violin concerto and quartet. He also composed his beautiful Symphony in D Minor for the same society, and altogether produced the profoundest effect upon art and artists in England. In regard to his music, the novelty of his harmonies, the exquisite delicacy of his subjects, and his never ceasing excitement could not fail to enchant the young musicians, many of whom became Spohr-mad, as they were a few years afterwards Weber-mad.

Spohr has made many subsequent visits to England, and is always received with the utmost veneration.

I have selected an appropriate example of his style, which I have no doubt will greatly delight you.

Early Quartett — two violins, alto, & cello	Spohr

Rossini

Our thoughts must turn from the <serious and thoughtful> {grave and conscientious} German composers to that brilliant genius, Rossini, who is also in the list of illustrious visitors to England. He arrived in England

1 Examples of music by these composers published in London may be found in Temperley, ed., *London Pianoforte School*, vols. 1–6.

2 In the printed syllabus, this is the penultimate item, between Weber and Mendelssohn.

3 Actually he arrived in February 1820.

in the year 1824,[1] in consequence of an engagement at the King's Theatre by which he was to be composer and director of the music, to superintend the performance of his own operas, and to produce a new one.

It is singular that this visit is the only one which I have to record as a failure, and I must confess that this fact interests me less than many others would. The speculation completely failed, the season was attended with enormous loss, and Rossini left England without having fulfilled his engagement to compose an opera.

He was however much patronised by private fashionable circles and took home with him much money.

My illustrations could not be complete without a specimen of this undoubted genius and erratic composer.

Duett[2]	Rossini

Weber

In 1826 Weber arrived in London to superintend the preparation and bringing out of Oberon at Covent Garden Theatre. He was received with great interest and the kindest attentions. He took up his abode with Sir George Smart at 91 Great Portland Street, in which house he in a few months afterwards breathed his last.

His letters to his wife are most interesting and fully explain the state of the English public in regard to him and his music. He says:

> At seven o'clock in the evening, we went to Covent Garden Theatre where Rob Roy was being performed. When the people found me out there they called out loudly for me, and insisted on having 'Der Freyschütz'. Could a man wish for more enthusiasm or more love?[3]

Is not this honourable testimony to the appreciation of the English people? What could be more valuable to us than this affecting acknowledgement on the part of the great genius.

Let me proceed with his testimony to our performers, equally valuable to us:

> And now my dear love, I can assure you that you may be quite at ease, both as to the singers and orchestra. Miss Paton is a singer of the first rank and will play Reiza divinely, Braham not less so, tho' in totally a different

1 Actually December 1823.

2 Called 'Duo' in the printed programme.

3 Letter of 7 April 1826. Another translation is to be found in Warrack, *Weber in London*, 13; Bennett may well have made his own translation of this and the other passages from a German edition.

> style. There are also several good tenors, and I really cannot see why the English singing should be abused. The singers have a perfectly good Italian education, fine voices, & expression. The orchestra is not remarkable, but still very good, and the choruses particularly so. In short, I feel quite at ease as to the fate of Oberon.[1]

Here is Weber's own statement of English art in 1826. One only sighs that he cannot be with us to witness our progress in 1858.

After the first performance of Oberon, he writes to his wife:

> Through God's grace and blessing, I have this evening met with the most complete success. The brilliancy and affecting nature of the triumph are indescribable. God alone be thanked for it! When I entered the orchestra, the whole of the house, which was filled to overflowing, rose up, and I was saluted by huzzas and waving of hats and handkerchiefs which I thought would never have done. They insisted on encoring the overtures. Every air was interrupted twice or thrice with bursts of applause. So much for this night.[2]

<Weber, while he was the delight of the small circle of musical friends with whom he lived, was disqualified by his feelings, habits and manners from sharing in the golden harvest so abundantly reaped by foreign favourites. On the 26th of May>[3]

How great was the influence of Weber's visit to us, many a living musician can bear witness. The impression made by him will long continue.

I have selected a song from Freyschütz.[4]

Song — 'No joy without its neighbour sorrow'[5]	Weber

Mendelssohn

The last great name in my list is the name of one most recently with us, Felix Mendelssohn Bartholdy – the delight of this country from the first moment he was known to it in 1829. How well he loved England, I have

1 Letter of 7 March 1826. See Warrack, *Carl Maria von Weber*, 350.

2 Letter dated '12 April [1826], 12.45 a.m.' See Warrack, *Weber in London*, 32.

3 Here the passage breaks off; Bennett then deleted it. Weber gave an unsuccessful concert on 26 May.

4 Altered in another hand, presumably for Sheffield, to: 'a very characteristic piece by this charming composer. Duett P.F.'

5 This is a translation of Agathe's aria 'Und ob die Wolke sie verhülle', which appeared in George Soane and Henry Bishop's adaptation of *Der Freischütz*, premiered at Drury Lane Theatre in 1824. I am grateful to Christina Fuhrmann for identifying this song. See Fuhrmann, 'Continental Opera Englished'.

had ample means of knowing. Even Weber was not more readily appreciated than Mendelssohn, who indeed by means of his stupendous oratorios has taken his place in the heart of English people second only to Handel.

Perhaps no illustrious visitor ever caused more excitement in England than did Mendelssohn, but his genius was universal. He was grand in all departments of the art, & as a man, most lovable <— ever ready to cheer and encourage the young musician>. The grand fact will ever remain – that he wrote for England the 'Elijah'.

I do not scruple to assert that Mendelssohn was more thoroughly appreciated by the English than by his own countrymen – and how much has English art gained by the never too oft repeated visits of this great man. We have had him as an example to our pianists, to our organists, to our conductors, to our composers of concert and chamber music, to the composers of church music, {to dramatic writers,} in fact there is no single department of the art which he did not represent and adorn.

One would greatly welcome a faithful biography of Felix Mendelssohn. No {musical} character which ever yet existed could shine more brilliantly than his.

Had I not known him so intimately, I might have trusted myself to talk more of his vast claims upon our affection. It is impossible to go deeper into the subject at this moment.[1] His public life is well known to you by means of the repeated performances of his colossal works. It is to be hoped that the English people will someday be equally well acquainted with his beautiful character as a man.

Some of his greatest contributions to art were composed when [he was] chapel master to the King of Prussia, and these are less known than many of his other compositions. Such was the music he wrote for Racine's Athalie, & to the Greek tragedies Antigone & Edipus. These were grand creations.

We will play for you the overture to Athalie, and in conclusion, I will just take a review of my subject, and I think we shall upon reflection be satisfied with the part which our country has taken in the course of music.

Grand Duett — Pianoforte[2]	Mendelssohn

---

[1] For further discussion of Bennett's feelings about Mendelssohn see Bennett, *Life*, 175–6.

[2] The overture to *Athalie*, arranged for four hands.

We may indeed reflect with pride and pleasure that our country has received and appreciated those great men who have been the subject of my lecture. It is no small thing to say that for England were composed the Oratorios of Handel, the Grand Symphonies of Haydn, the Oberon of Weber, that the English taste stimulated Gluck to his new form of opera, that Mozart wrote for us, that Spohr has devoted his talents to us, that Mendelssohn, as I have before stated, wrote his Elijah for us.

May we not take all these facts as evidence of a keen musical perception in the English character, and that our nation is quite as able to decide upon what is great in art, as any other nation. The first Napoleon called us a nation of shopkeepers. We have at any rate always kept a considerable warehouse for the fine arts. Where is the appreciation of such a genius as Mendelssohn amongst the French? Do we tolerate the extravagance of the present German school?[1]

There are two names which I should indeed have been proud, could we have included them in our list, John Seb. Bach and Beethoven. But even Beethoven was intimately connected with art in England, and wrote for the Philharmonic Society his last great symphony.

I feel that I have done very imperfect justice to my subject, <but I trust on some future occasion to work out my plan more effectively.

In the meantime I shall probably be able at my fourth lecture to repair many omissions which I am conscious of having made this evening, owing to the largeness of my subject and the limit of my time.>

1 It is noteworthy that Bennett passed over not only Liszt and Wagner but also Berlioz, Chopin, and Verdi. All had made substantial appearances in England before 1858. Wagner's visit would be mentioned in the fourth lecture (see p. 77 below).

3

On the Vocal Music of England

London Institution, 29 April 1858

The ground over which I propose to travel this evening has been oft trodden before.[1] No wonder: lecturers on music have quickly discovered the strong point connected with the art and English composers, and it seems that the position will be rather strengthened than weakened by continuous and wider enquiries into the subject, aided by new matter and material for which we have to be grateful to zealous lovers of English vocal music, and enterprising editors.

Had not this my 3rd lecture been intimately bound up with the series, such series having especial regard to English music and English musicians, I could [still] not have resisted the temptation of devoting one of my evenings to the praises of those of my countrymen who have for ever rescued England from obscurity in the history of the art – who, indeed, have secured for her a most honourable place among the writers of vocal music in past and present times.

Before I proceed further, it will be necessary for me to explain what I mean to include under the title of 'Vocal Music of England'.

Let me say at once that I have not the slightest intention of taking the subject of the so-called 'national music' in hand, or of embroiling myself in the discussions upon the origin and authorship of any certain tune or melody adopted by the English: for instance, as to who shall be awarded the laurel for 'God Save the Queen', whether Dr. John Bull or another. There is a periodical run in the newspapers upon this very subject, and as I have not heard anything about it lately, I suppose it to be nearly due again, when every provincial paper in the kingdom will let us know that some additional facts have been brought to light as to who is the

[1] An impression of the popularity of lectures on music in London in these years can be gained from *Répertoire international de la presse musicale* [*RIPM*]: *The Musical World 1836–1865*, 8 (Ann Arbor: UMI Press, 1997), 3037–8.

composer of the royal tune, but which facts will most assuredly tend to increase the mystery.

There is also a large class of vocal music but little connected with music as an art, which however has given boundless gratification in past times, and no doubt much of it continues to delight in the present day. I allude to the characteristic songs of ——————[1] Carey & Dibdin. These I must content myself to dismiss with mere mention.

I make a much greater sacrifice in excluding from my lecture any specimens of church music, in which branch we may be said to rival any country in Europe. It must be obvious however that the subject is far too comprehensive and far too serious to be taken in hand as a mere adjunct, and most willingly would I on some future occasion devote a set of lectures to this subject alone.

Fortunately some of the great men who would have been prominently brought forward in connection with church music, being also composers of secular music, will still be represented this evening: such are Byrd, Gibbons, Purcell, & others more modern.

William Byrd born in about the year 1538, was a pupil of the celebrated Tallis, and is said to have been brought up in the music school of St. Paul's Cathedral. He composed principally sacred works. His masses are presumed to have been written for St. Paul's Cathedral during the reign of Queen Mary. The great number of his ecclesiastical compositions to Latin words, and the several portions of the Romish ritual which he so frequently set to music and published late in life, seem to pronounce Byrd a zealous adherent to the Roman Catholic religion. He must, however, have subsequently followed the example of his master, Tallis, and conformed to the church establishment.[2]

Byrd's pupil, Thomas Morley, speaks of him as 'his most loving master, never without reverence to be named of musicians.'[3] I must remind myself that I am not introducing Byrd this evening in his light as a church composer, and therefore shall only quote, from Dr Rimbault's preface to one of the new editions of Byrd's works, an anecdote which will connect Byrd with the specimen of his secular works which I have been able to find for illustration this evening. Dr Rimbault says:

1 Bennett here drew a long line, as if he planned to add other names to the list of composers. It is not clear why he 'dismissed' the songs of Henry Carey and Charles Dibdin, who are generally considered to be among the best 18th-century English song composers.

2 On the opposite page, Bennett wrote : 'Tallis & Bird [sic], who were equally admirable in their musical production & execution, are now only known and revered by the choirs — Burney [*General History*] — page 441, vol. 2.' His remarks about Byrd's career are, of course, largely mistaken.

3 We have not found the source of this quotation.

> In a volume of the Talbot papers preserved in the Herald's College I have discovered a very interesting allusion to one of Byrd's most beautiful compositions. It is in a letter written by the Earl of Worcester to the Earl of Shrewsbury, September 19, 1602, and the passage is as follows: 'We are frolic here in court, much dancing in the privy chamber of country dances before the Queen's Majesty, who is exceedingly pleased therewith: Irish tunes are at this time most pleasing, but in winter "Lullaby" an old song of Mr Bird's, will be more in request as I think.' This song must have enjoyed considerable popularity previous to the year 1602.[1]

I am delighted to have found it in order to increase the interest of my illustration.

Lullaby ['Lullaby, my sweet little baby']	Byrd

In Kiesewetter's History of Music (a modern German work), we find the following acknowledgment of the English composers of this period. I merely record it as a pleasing sign that foreign writers begin to find they must include England sometimes.

Speaking of music in this epoch he says:

> The school that existed at this time in England had Tallis & his pupil Byrd, both organists to Queen Elizabeth, whose works may indeed be placed in juxtaposition with the best of their contemporaries. Toward the end of this epoch, and partly in the beginning of the following, there flourished in the same country Dr John Bull, and a multitude of popular madrigal writers, whose very pleasing works have now become known in Germany by means of a new edition lately published in London, in which among other names we find those of Bateson, Barnett, Dowland, Gibbon[s], Morley, Ward, Wilby, Weelkes and many others, the memory of which has been revived by Hawkins and Burney.[2]

It is remarkable that this German historian, although giving long lists of musicians in each century, including the above, has omitted the name of Purcell. It is still more extraordinary that his translator should not have reminded him of the fact.

Time will not allow me to give you many specimens of that remarkable era in English music when flourished our great madrigal writers. Quoting from Hogarth's Musical History:

[1] Quoted from Rimbault, 'Memoir', 9, with the last sentence reduced. 'Lullaby, my sweet little baby', a five-voice consort song, was printed in Byrd's *Psalmes, Sonets and Songs* (London, 1588).

[2] Quoted from Kiesewetter, *History*, 177–8, with trivial alterations. The edition referred to is that of the Musical Antiquarian Society. Its 19 volumes (1841–48) included all the composers mentioned by Kiesewetter, if we assume that 'Barnett' is a misnomer for John Bennet. Four of them were devoted to works by Purcell.

> Most of the great Italian composers of the sixteenth century distinguished themselves by their madrigals; particularly Palestrina, Luca Marenzio, Giovanni Croce, Stradella, Steffani, and others. About the period of which we speak, the madrigals of these composers began to be adapted to English words and thus the foundation was laid for a school in which we soon rivalled, if not surpassed, the Italians themselves.[1]

These beautiful productions, in the age[2] in which they appeared, were the music chiefly resorted to as a recreation in England. To sing in parts was an accomplishment held to be indispensable in a well educated lady or gentleman.

At a social meeting, when the madrigal books were laid on the table, everybody was expected to take a share in the harmony; and any one who declined on the score of inability was looked upon with some contempt, as rude & low-bred.

In Morley's Introduction to Practical Music, which, after the fashion of the day, is in the form of a dialogue, the scholar is made to seek instruction in consequence of a mortification he had met with {the previous evening}, owing to his ignorance of music.[3]

During the decline of music, in the 17th century, vocal harmony fell into neglect, in which state it remained until it was revived by the establishment of the Madrigal Society in 1741, and by other associations for the performance of part-music, which have been since formed not only in London, but in all parts of the kingdom.

I have chosen two perfect specimens of madrigals, one by Orlando Gibbons, the other by Wilbye. Before you hear these compositions, I will just say a very few words upon the personal and artistic life of the two great composers.

Orlando Gibbons was a native of the town of Cambridge,[4] and born in the year 1583. At the age of 21 he was appointed organist of the Chapel Royal and in 1622 (along with Dr Heyther) obtained the degree of doctor of music, in the university of Oxford. Three years after this, being ordered to go to Canterbury for the purpose of attending the marriage solemnity between King Charles 1st and Henrietta of France (for which he had composed the music), he was seised with the small pox, and died

1 Hogarth, *Musical History*, 41.

2 From the words 'in which', the rest of this paragraph and the next two are in Mary Bennett's hand, except for the words 'the previous evening', inserted later by Bennett. See p. 19, Plate 4.

3 This is how Morley introduces the teacher–student dialogue which is the form of his famous work. See Morley, *Introduction*, 9.

4 Gibbons was a actually born in Oxford, but was educated at Cambridge as a chorister.

there at the age of 45. He was buried in the cathedral church of that city. In 1612 he published 'Madrigals in 4 parts, for voices and viols.'

This evening I present him only as a composer in this style of music, having already expressed my regret that the plan of my lecture debars me from giving specimens of that style in which he stands so preeminent.

Madrigal, 'Sweet honey-sucking Bees'	Wilbye
Madrigal, 'The Silver Swan'	Gibbons

Of Wilbye, it has been said that if Luca Marenzio was rightly styled the most charming Swan of Italy, so was Wilbye the Swan of England as a madrigal writer.[1] In the preface to his madrigals, presented for the first time in score to his countrymen under the editorship of the accomplished musician, Mr Turle, organist of Westminster Abbey, we are told that 'no record remains of Wilbye, save that imperishable one – his works'. In the absence of authentic information, Mr Turle quotes from one of Professor Taylor's lectures at Gresham College: 'There dwelt nearly opposite to Sir Thomas Gresham's house in Broad street, a musician of rare endowment, John Wilbye, by name.'[2]

Wilbye is principally known as a writer of madrigals: and these compositions, which were habitually resorted to at the time in which they were written as the social recreation of the festive board, continue to charm all lovers of English vocal harmony to the present hour.

Henry Purcell[3] was born in 1658 and was appointed organist of Westminster Abbey at 18 years of age. At 24 he was nominated as one of the organists of the Chapel Royal; after this he produced many compositions for the church & chapel of which he was organist, [and] from this time his anthems were procured with eagerness and heard with pious rapture wherever they could be performed. Nor was he long suffered to devote his talents exclusively to the service of the church. He was very early in life solicited to compose for the stage and the chamber, and in compositions for the theatre, though the colourings and effects of an orchestra were then but little known; yet as he employed them more than his predecessors, & gave to the voice a melody more interesting and impassioned than during that century had been heard in this country or even perhaps

1 'If Luca Marenzio was rightly styled "il più dolce cigno d'Italia", to John Wilbye may correctly be awarded a similar station as a Madrigal writer, in reference not only to his English, but perhaps to his other great European contemporaries.' Turle, 'Introduction', 1.

2 Quoted from James Turle, 'Introduction', which in turn took the passage from Taylor, *Gresham College Lectures*, Lecture 3, p. 43.

3 The entire section on Purcell is in Mary Bennett's hand. In fact, Purcell was born in 1659.

in Italy, he soon became the light and darling of the nation, and in the several species of chamber music which he attempted, whether sonatas for instruments, cantatas, songs, ballads, or catches for the voice, he so far surpassed whatever our country had produced or imported before that all others' musical compositions seemed to have been instantly consigned to oblivion.

Purcell's theatrical compositions (bearing in mind his contributions to church music and the shortness of his life) will surprise by their multiplicity. Thanks to the English Musical Antiquarian Society, his extraordinary dramatic work 'Dido and Æneas', a tragic opera in three acts, was first printed entire in 1840.

In this work we find specimens of musical power not inferior to Bach and Mendelssohn. Indeed one {short} example which I shall now offer you must strike all connoisseurs of the Bach school with astonishment at the close resemblance it bears in form, sentiment, and manner with the Crucifixus in the Great Mass in B Minor of the renowned German.

Song from 'Dido and Aeneas'[1]	Purcell

From the Dictionary of Musicians:[2]

From the death of Purcell to that of Arne, a period of more than four-score years, no candidate for musical fame among our countrymen had appeared who was equally admired by the nation at large.

It[3] appears that Arne was an Eton boy, and intended for the law. But his love for music operated upon him too powerfully even while at Eton, either for his own peace or that of his companions, for with a miserable cracked common flute, he used to torment them night and day when not obliged to attend at school.

In 1738 Arne established his reputation as a lyric composer by the admirable manner in which he set Milton's 'Comus'. In this masque or work, he introduced the light, airy, original and pleasing melody, wholly different from that of Purcell or Handel, whom hitherto all English composers had either pillaged or imitated.

It was in 1762 that Arne quitted that style of melody to be found in 'Comus' and furnished Vauxhall [Gardens] & the whole kingdom with such songs as improved and polished our national taste.

<I must confess, in reviewing the music of Arne in the last few days, I

1 Undoubtedly this song was Dido's lament, 'When I am laid in earth'.

2 These words are followed by a gap of two or three lines, which perhaps Bennett intended to fill with a quotation from Sainsbury's *Dictionary*. The passage about Arne at Eton, further down, is taken from the *Dictionary*, 1:28.

3 From here to the end of the section on Attwood the text is in Mary Bennett's hand.

have been agreeably surprised to meet with such purity of musical thought and feeling.> There can be no doubt that his natural and unaffected music will long retain its place in the hearts of every lover of English music.

I would particularly call your attention to the exquisite cadence at the end of each verse in the song which I am now going to offer you.

Song, 'Where the Primrose' [from *Eliza*, 1754]	Arne

In Hogarth's Musical History it is said:

> The glee may be considered as peculiar to England. Other countries may afford scattered specimens of this description of music, but it is in this country only that it has engaged the attention of the most distinguished composers. The word glee as indicating a particular form of musical composition appears to have been first used in a work published by Playford in 1667 consisting of dialogues, glees, airs, and ballads of two, three, & four voices.[1]

By general consent Samuel Webbe [the elder] is placed at the head of the list of our glee composers. He is the author of above a hundred glees & part songs. Associated with him are Dr Callcott, Stevens, Horsley, and others whom I have not sufficient time to honour.

In giving you specimens from Webb[e], Callcott, & Horsley I feel that I am doing full justice to the school.

Glee, 'Come live with me' [1771]	Webbe
Glee, 'The Friars of Orders Gray' [c.1795]	Callcott
Glee, 'See the Chariot' [1807]	Horsley

Attwood

There is one name [which] whilst still connected with the glee school links itself onto the more pliant and rhythmical compositions of later times. I allude to Thomas Attwood. I shall always embrace every opportunity of paying my tribute to the merit of this polished & graceful musician.

Attwood also suffers from my plan of this evening, as not being considered as a church composer. As organist of St. Paul's & composer

[1] Quoted from Hogarth, *Musical History*, 407. The publication in question was Book II of Playford's *Catch that Catch Can* (see bibliography). This passage undermines Bennett's earlier statement (p. 61) that 'during the decline of music, in the 17th century, vocal harmony fell into neglect.'

to the Chapel Royal, he has produced on special occasions several sacred works of surpassing merit, but as a secular composer alone he should be known in every English house where music is practised.

He brought to the English school the influence of ideas which he had derived from his master Mozart. Well do I remember as a boy, after taking part in the very glee which we are now about to perform, hearing Mendelssohn take up the theme at the pianoforte with the greatest delight <and expatiating on and> developing the subject to the exquisite pleasure of Attwood himself & all around.[1]

Previous to the glee I think it but justice to Attwood to offer you a specimen of his solo writing, a most beautiful song which I know to have been his own especial favorite.

Song, 'Marraton and Yaratilda'	Attwood
Glee, 'The Curfew'	Attwood

Our list of good names is not yet exhausted. There is one name indeed which deserves more than passing attention – and I sincerely regret that my limits will not allow me to do it anything like justice.[2] I allude to the truly English composer, Bishop, who sustained the national school of dramatic music for upward of a quarter of a century, and who during that time produced about five and thirty original works beside assisting in many others. Bishop's music is so well known to English people that I need not take up your time in expatiating upon its merits. I content myself with the opportunity now afforded to testify to the genius of this distinguished man, who made his only failure when he allowed himself to be set up as the rival to Weber, after which circumstance his career as a composer seemed to close.[3]

Glee, 'Now Day's retiring lamp'[4]	Bishop

Goss

As time moves on, I must proceed more rapidly and bring my remarks and illustrations closer together. Indeed as I am now about to speak of living vocal writers only, my remarks need be but few. There is no doubt

1 This episode took place in 1833. See Bennett, *Life*, 31.

2 The text continues 'But your acquaintance with the', but then Bennett crossed this out and began the next sentence.

3 This refers to Bishop's *Aladdin*, which opened at Drury Lane on 29 April 1826 in an unsuccessful attempt to draw some of the public away from Weber's *Oberon* at Covent Garden.

4 Probably 'Now by day's retiring lamp', a quintet from Bishop and Ware's *Don John, or The Two Violettas* (1821).

that you in your own minds will do full justice to those authors who being now with us are giving their talents and examples in maintaining the purity of the art.

Amongst the most accomplished musicians of the present day is John Goss, the organist of St. Paul's. He is both a profound scholar and an imaginative musician, and one cannot but regret that this composer does not come more prominently before the public. His last great work was the funeral service for the Duke of Wellington, a work worthy to be placed side by side with those of the greatest of church writers.[1]

You will experience great pleasure in listening to the beautiful little composition by this author, 'There is beauty on the mountain.'

Glee, 'There is beauty on the mountain'	Goss

Barnett, Loder, Macfarren, Smart

I cannot conclude my programme of illustrations without including one or two more specimens of our best English vocal writers – writers full of genius and enthusiasm, who with the necessary encouragement of the English public would prove themselves worthy of any age.

It is indeed a misfortune that whilst the London public can afford to support two Italian operas, every attempt to rear an English opera has entirely failed.[2] I cannot suggest the reasons which invariably lead to this result; one thing only I know, that the fault is not the lack of genius amongst our dramatic composers. Where is the modern Italian composer who could compete with either Barnett, Loder, Smart or Macfarren? And even many others?

Is the matter of a national opera ever to remain a hopeless question?

In the selections I have made from the vocal works of the writers whose names I have last mentioned, I have been obliged to consider my means of illustration, rather than the hope of doing these composers full justice.

Trio, 'This magic-wove scarf' [from *The Mountain Sylph* (1834)]	Barnett
Duett, 'The Convent Bell' [1855]	Henry Smart
Madrigal, 'King Charles II'[3]	Macfarren

1 Goss wrote a dirge, 'And the king said to all the people', and an anthem, 'If we believe that Jesus died', for Wellington's funeral on 18 November 1852. These were by no means his latest works in 1858, however.

2 For details of the attempts to found national opera companies in this period see Temperley, 'English Romantic Opera'; Hurd, 'Opera: 1834–1865', 307–10. For a list of operas premiered see Biddlecombe, *English Opera from 1834 to 1864*, 332–7.

3 Probably the madrigal 'Maidens, never go a-wooing' from Macfarren's opera *King Charles II* (1849).

Conclusion

In conclusion may I be allowed to make one suggestion. The cultivation of music, in this or any other country, is in a very great measure in the hands of the public, and it is the public which decides the direction of art, whether for good or for evil. Composers like others have to gain their bread by their vocation. 'They who live to please, must please to live.' If the public will not encourage the full development of their talents, and [will] be ever more content with the shell than the kernel, can it astonish anyone that our music shops are teeming with light productions rather than with thoughtful music[?] You will remember how strongly I expressed myself upon the subject of home music in my first lecture, and I cannot resist appealing to you to help the art & thereby the composers of England to maintain that position to which, I have proved to you this evening, they are so justly entitled in the music schools of Europe. This can be done most effectively by the style of music adopted in the education of those for whom you are responsible.

Such musicians as I have brought forward this evening should be known and appreciated by all English people, not only for what they have done for the gratification of past times, not only for the gratification which we of the present day may receive from them if we will, but also that their compositions will supply delight & enjoyment to our children's children, destined as they are to remain as models of art and science for ages to come.

4

On the General Prospects of Music in England[1]

London Institution, 6 May 1858

I propose this evening to take you with me on a visit to the principal schools of modern music in Europe, as they exist at the present moment – glancing occasionally at the past; comparing former times with the present, whether to the advantage or disadvantage of those countries which will come under our notice; interspersing my remarks with such illustration as will do no injustice to the composers whom I shall bring forward; and in conclusion to say a few words upon the prospects of music in England in the future.

I trust that wherever I shall feel it my duty to point out any symptom of decay in countries long and deservedly celebrated for their might and influence in upholding the art in its integrity, I may express myself in language which could not possibly give offence, and although couched in words of regret should be void of all tone of contempt or forgetfulness of what we, as English people, owe to our foreign neighbours.

In my second lecture, 'On the visits of foreign musicians to England', it was with the sincerest pleasure that I brought forward to your notice the vast debt of gratitude which was due to those giants of the art who aided our progress by their presence and example, and by their contributions to our musical stores; and although in a subsequent discourse, I was enabled with a very clear conscience to present England in a light in which I think her little, if at all, inferior to other musical nations, we

1 Bound in with this lecture is a sheet containing a rejected introduction. It reads as follows: 'To discover my plot <to you> at once, and bring you to the end of my story before I have fairly begun it, I am conscientiously of opinion that England (which for long past has been steadily preparing itself to protect musical art, when endangered by the fascination of false prophets) will, sooner than foreign critics dream of, be that country to which all musicians of the true stamp will appeal to for <refuge> {a just verdict}. I am quite aware that this is an assertion which will require' Here the passage breaks off.

must not, indeed we cannot overlook the fact that in many points she is still sadly deficient, and, at present, but little prepared to represent the art generally. I should only bring ridicule upon myself, and injury to my professional brethren, were I to attempt to prove that England can do all which is done by foreign nations. That she will do so at some future time I have not the slightest doubt. But enough of this for the present. I am only anxious to set an example of candour and honesty to some of the critics on the other side of the water, who, as you have already heard me say several times, contrive to leave England entirely out of the question when taking up their inspired pens to dilate upon art progress. There is an immense amount of trash which finds its way into the compositor's hands in these times upon the subject of {the so called} art progress.

Within the last few days, I have been amused (and something more) by reading a book emanating from a distinguished German musical critic, and which has been honored with three English translations. Speaking of Weber, and his opera of Euryanthe, he says, 'In none of his works has Weber proved himself so fertile as in this; no where else has he, or any of his predecessors or contemporaries, adapted so ingeniously and happily the tone of expression to the time and place to which the drama refers. But by this time', continues the writer, 'the thoughts and ideas of the people had already taken another direction. Neither Weber nor his librettist had been able to distinguish between that which is transient and perishable, and that which lives for ever: Euryanthe was, and remains a failure. But {he concludes that} though this opera met with no success upon the stage, it will for ever hold a prominent position in the development of our art, as one of the most energetic and' (pray mark the patronising language) 'praiseworthy attempts at truthful delineation.'[1]

In another portion of this curious piece of musical literature, we are told that Mendelssohn, in writing the music to Antigone, did it 'with intelligence, tact, and great talent. But <he has as little succeeded in doing justice to the ancient poet as our musical art can succeed, and> he has degraded this, our art, by employing it for purposes which not only limit its powers and resources, but actually ensnare it into a want of truthfulness.'[2]

But we have a journey before us this evening which we have not yet begun. So, let us leave Dr Bernard Marx with the very few disciples he

1 Quoted from Marx, *Music of the Nineteenth Century*, 63. Bennett chose to leave out the explanatory sentence following the words 'taken another direction': 'The middle age, with its spectral apparitions and mysterious voices, its mingled idolisation and degradation of women, the whole circle of its ideas and characters had become strange to the people.' Ironically, Marx's views about music were ultimately conservative and agreed in many respects with Bennett's.

2 Quoted from Marx, *Music of the Nineteenth Century*, 67. The passage in angle brackets was correctly quoted from the source, but later deleted by Bennett.

will ever gain in England; for we know how to estimate both Weber & Mendelssohn.

Now to begin with Italy, that land which has given to us Palestrina, Luca Marenzio, Carissimi, the two Scarlattis, Corelli, Festa & many others scarcely less brilliant. Should not, I say, that land be looked upon with grateful feelings and admiration by all those who are sensible to any charm in music? Did not the Italians for centuries uphold the grandeur of the art?

One cannot but lament that the Italian composers of the present day are more actively employed in subserving the demands of fashion than in following the true ends of art. Here indeed is a case of degeneracy which it would be affectation to disguise. Step by step has musical art lowered itself among those who were formerly its most vigilant and powerful champions.

What would Luca Marenzio say, could he rise from his grave, to the ragged chorus {part} writing to be found in the modern Italian opera, the main portion of which seems to be rather the work of the copyist than the composer – nothing but what is technically called 'filling-up', which any tyro could accomplish.

But, for this state of things, the fashionable public is in a great measure to blame. When the great artist of the night has performed the loved aria, the house is released from enchantment, and in a few moments the general murmur gives way to a confusion of tongues more resembling the arena of an auction than the palace of high art. Of what avail (so would a modern Italian {composer} defend himself) to step in with a regularly constructed chorus, grammatically written and skillfully developed under such circumstances? I cannot undertake to answer the question. I only know that these gross inconsistencies in what assumes to be a representation of grand opera have long prevented genuine musicians from taking any interest in the majority of lyrical dramatic performances.

My present aim is merely to include a review of the modern schools of music in Europe. But in justice to Italy, I must give you one specimen of the starting point of grand opera, selected from that epoch when the institution took its new shape – which new shape some attribute to the great German, Gluck, and others to the Italian composer whose name is first in my programme of illustration this evening.

May I say a few words upon Piccini {and his immediate successors}?

[**Piccini**]

Piccini[1] was a native of Naples. He was born in 1728, and educated at the conservatory of that city, which, under the direction of the celebrated masters, Leo and Durante, was then the greatest music school in Europe.

[1] From here to the end of the section on Méhul the text is in Mary Bennett's hand.

He wrote many operas for Naples and Rome but did not acquire his European fame till after his arrival at Paris, when he had nearly reached the age of fifty.

'Se il ciel mi divide' [aria from *Alessandro nell' Indie*]	Piccini[1]

The German composer Gluck (whom I have on a former occasion introduced to your notice) had arrived there a few years before. They were placed in a position of direct competition, both being employed to write for the same theatre, the Académie Royale de Musique, or Grand Opera as it is called, and the operas of both were in the French language,[2] though they are now known throughout Europe chiefly through the medium of Italian versions. Their rivalry caused the most violent feud known in musical history. The partisans of the Italian and German[3] schools rallied round the representative of each; and as these partisans included every class of Parisian society, royalty not excepted, a civil war raged among them which often broke the ties of family & friendship. Each of them, however, received effectual support from his adherents and the works of both were alternately & successfully performed. Both [were] musical reformers, and both did much for the progress of the art. But in this respect the labours of Gluck were more efficacious than those of his rival; and hence, while the beautiful music of Piccini is forgotten, the more original works of Gluck still serve as models to the dramatic composer.

Paisiello[4]

The contemporary of Cimarosa, like Piccini, was a disciple of the Neapolitan school. He was born at Tarento in the kingdom of Naples in 1741, and during a long life which terminated in 1816, he produced a vast number of operas for all the Italian theatres which spread his fame throughout Europe. None of them now keeps possession of the stage; but much of his music is still preserved in the form of detached airs, duets, and concerted pieces, and will always charm by its singular simplicity, grace & expression.

1 This musical illustration is not listed in the lecture text, but it is printed in the advance syllabus. The aria gained popularity in England when it was reused in the 1786 pasticcio *Didone abbandonata*.

2 The operas concerned were Piccini's *Roland* and Gluck's *Armide*, both produced in 1777.

3 At the time Gluck's efforts were perceived as an attempt to renew and modernise French opera, not particularly German in character. See Rushton, 'Gluck: Paris, 1774–9'.

4 Modern spelling. Bennett consistently spelled the name 'Paesiello'.

The little air which I shall introduce as a specimen of Paisiello will give a good idea of his light and comic vein.

Duet, 'Pandolfetto graziosetto' [from *I zingari in fiera*]	Paisiello

[Verdi]

Passing over Rossini, and his more immediate successors Bellini and [Donizetti,][1] whose operas have so long engrossed our musical stage, both Italian and English, that they have become familiar to everybody, I shall come at once to the reigning favourite of the day, Verdi, who notwithstanding his immeasurable inferiority, has gained a degree of popularity exceeding that of Rossini himself. During the last twenty years he has produced a numerous series of operas, all of the tragic or serious class; and as he is only of middle age, he may if the present rage continues, produce as many more.

His principal works are the Lombardi, Ernani, the Due Foscari, Rigoletto, the Trovatore, and the Traviata. The last two have been so successful in this country that they have almost monopolised our Italian opera-houses, it having been no uncommon thing, last season, for the one or the other of them to be performed at Her Majesty's Theatre and the Royal Italian Opera the same evening. Music so generally popular cannot be wholly destitute of merit: and Verdi, though he has no depth and little constructive power, has at least a vein of pleasing Italian melody which catches the popular ear, so that his pretty tunes are ground on barrel organs in every street in London. I must give one specimen of a composer so renowned at present throughout the whole musical world, and I take an air from the Trovatore, one of the happiest of his melodies.

Aria, 'Il balen del suo sorriso', from Il Trovatore	Verdi

[France: Méhul]

Speaking of France, it is singular that a country so near to our own should have so little sympathy with other nations on musical subjects.[2] In proof of this I may mention three remarkable facts: the only oratorio of

[1] Here Bennett left a blank.

[2] The manuscript contains a separate sheet on which is written what was evidently a rejected introduction to this section. It reads: 'Coming to France, may I ask, "Shall that country which is impervious to the influence of foreign musicians, maintaining its character with most remarkable obstinacy, be allowed in its turn to influence the art abroad[?"] I believe not. In acknowledging the claim [that] some [credit?] is [due?] to

Handel ever performed in Paris has been The Messiah a very few times; Haydn's great work the Creation has been performed only twice, the first time on the memorable night nearly 60 years ago when Napoleon (then first Consul), on his way to hear it, was nearly destroyed by the famous infernal machine; and the second time some eight or ten years ago; and lastly that one act of Mendelssohn's Elijah was lately produced with a great flourish of trumpets as if it were some wonderful achievement. Nevertheless I cannot deny to the French that they possess an exquisite school of their own, remarkable for a light, airy grace which in fact is in unison with the character of the people. Any country might be proud of such names as Méhul, Boieldieu, Auber, and of the works which they have produced such as Joseph, La dame blanche, and Masaniello, and we cannot but be envious of the great seminary, where the genius of these men has been fostered: the Conservatoire of Paris, a magnificent institution liberally and entirely supported by the government and in which the most eminent professors of every branch of the art give their services without cost to the students.

It seemed to me, before introducing the very modern French composers, that you should have an opportunity of hearing a specimen of the older school. I will therefore submit to you an air from the opera of Joseph by Méhul.

Song, 'Ere Infancy's bud'[1]	Méhul

Berlioz & Gounod

Amongst the composers of the present time in France who attract the greatest attention are Berlioz and Gounod – both writers for the theatre and the concert room. Speaking first of Berlioz, to whom without doubt must be allowed the character of a sincere and devoted artist, I may say that he has produced many symphonies and operas, about the merit of which, there has been much difference of opinion. But it cannot be doubted that his treatment of a great orchestra is masterly in the extreme.

With regard to Gounod, of whom I am obliged to confess I know less, he has already interested the musical world by production of several works of <genius> {importance}, both sacred and secular. There are many who foretell a bright future for this young artist.

French composers, such as Herold, Boieldieu[?], Auber, and at the present' Here the passage breaks off; the last few words are barely legible.

1 'A peine au sortir de l'enfance', from *Joseph*, with English words by H. M. Milner.

His opera of 'Sappho', produced some few years since[1] at Covent Garden Theatre, had not much success, its comparative failure being ascribed by the friends of Gounod (and perhaps justly) to the defects of the drama rather than of the music. Mr Hullah has produced some of Gounod's sacred compositions with gratifying success.

In illustration of these two composers, I will perform a piece from the oratorio of the 'Infancy of Christ' by Berlioz & a detached song full of grace and feeling by Gounod.

Song, 'Venice'[2]	Gounod
Song, from 'The Infancy of Christ'	Berlioz

Belgium[3]

To the honor of Belgium be it stated that its government maintains a conservatory of music at Brussels, which admits students without regard to nationality, payment, or numbers. I could scarcely believe this when it was first told me, but subsequent enquiries made upon the spot have removed all doubt upon the matter.

This is an example which might be so easily followed by England.

Belgium, up to this day, has remained one of the great supports of music. It is still rich in musical talent, especially in instrumental performers, including Madame Pleyel, De Beriot, Servais, Vieuxtemps and a host of others.

Solo Violin, 'Fantasia-Caprice' [Op. 11][4]	Vieuxtemps

I thought it would be a great pleasure to you to hear a violin solo composed by a Belgian artist.

Holland

Of the present state of music in Holland I am enabled to speak by experience. I have been a delighted witness of the musical festivities of that country, and have also had opportunity to become acquainted with the striking ability of many of the young Dutch composers.

1 In 1851, in Italian translation.

2 Probably *Venise* ('Dans Venise la voyage'). However, no publication of this song earlier than 1863 has been found, when it appeared in Paris as No. 9 of *Vingt mélodies pour chant et piano*, [1er recueil].

3 The sections on Belgium and Holland are written in Mary Bennett's hand.

4 This work is for violin and piano.

I am not aware whether the Dutch government affords any direct aid to music and musicians, but I know that the Dutch people themselves make important sacrifices to this end.

There is existing in Holland a musical society which is perfectly unique. This society is denominated 'The Society for the Furtherance of Music in the Netherlands',[1] understood of course not to include Belgium.

As I have the honor to be a member of this interesting and highly useful association, I can furnish you with some very important information with regard to it, and I sincerely wish that England with all its wealth would carry out a similar plan.

The institution of which I speak has its headquarters at Amsterdam, and its branches in every important town in the kingdom. No genuine native talent is allowed to pass unheeded or neglected. Young composers are by the society provided with means to pursue their studies under the best guidance. They are rewarded with money prizes. Their compositions are printed by the society if found worthy of such distinction, having been first submitted to the most eminent musical judges in Europe, whose opinion alone decides the point. At the annual musical festivals the best specimens of the young composers are performed before the public.

One of the most zealous and rising of the young Dutch musicians is Verhulst, music director at Rotterdam.[2] He is a musician who deserves to be widely known, and from his works I have culled a little specimen which I trust may do him justice.

'Sacred Song'	Verhulst

Before I come to Germany, there is one German name which has so connected itself with various countries that I scarcely know where to give it its proper place. I can best describe my difficulty by saying that Meyerbeer, being a German, writes operas in the Italian manner chiefly for the French stage.

It would be an omission on my part if I did not give you the advantage of hearing a few works from the pen of this distinguished man, who

1 The Maatschappij tot Bevordering der Toonkunst was founded in 1829, the year before Belgium gained independence from Dutch rule. Bennett was elected a member in 1839 and had reviewed a number of compositions submitted to the Society for publication. One of his own compositions, the Toccata for piano, Op. 38, was first published in the Society's Album for 1854. (Temperley, *London Pianoforte School*, 18, xxv; Williamson, *Catalogue*, 202.)

2 Johannes Josephus Herman Verhulst (1816–91), an exact contemporary of Bennett's, had become a close friend during his visit to Leipzig in 1842. See Bennett, *Life*, 121, 235.

combines in his genius the characteristics of the various dramatic schools in Europe.

Song, 'Nobil donna è tanto onesta'[1]	Meyerbeer

Germany

You will not require me to give you any lengthened remarks upon the state of the musical art in Germany, as it existed up to that period when it had to deplore the loss of its brightest luminary, the illustrious Mendelssohn. In my discourse upon the 'Visits of Foreign Musicians to England' our time was principally occupied with the great German composers, of whom he was the last. I have therefore to confine my observations to that short period which has since elapsed. I wish I could look with pleasure upon what has taken place in recent times in Germany, but this is impossible. {In speaking of our chances for the future we must refer to our musical friends abroad.}

Germany is now divided into musical sects – some being Schumanites, some Wagnerites, some adopting both, and happily, others still remaining stedfast in the true faith.

[Schumann]

Robert Schumann, my dear personal friend,[2] I cannot allow to be confounded with the musicians of the present romantic school, who are endeavouring to turn day into night. I know Schumann to have been a sincere lover of all that was pure and great in music; his pen has oft shown his appreciation of the great masters. I am inclined to believe that Schumann's present extraordinary reputation is rather due to the superabundant enthusiasm of his disciples than to his own powers. He would have been the last person in the world to have wished himself exalted above Mendelssohn, as has been done by his indiscreet admirers. I have sat daily for six or 8 months in years gone by at the Table d'hôte in Leipzig with Mendelssohn, Schumann, and others, and I am witness to the delight with which Schumann husbanded every minute spent in the company of our illustrious friend.

1 'Une dame noble et sage', a cavatina from *Les Huguenots*, here in Italian translation.

2 From here to the end of the lecture the text is in Mary Bennett's hand. For Schumann's English reputation at this time and Bennett's conflicted opinion of his music see Temperley, 'Schumann and Sterndale Bennett', 214–16.

Selections from the pianoforte pieces 'à quatre mains'	Schumann
'Schlümmerlied', Slumber Song [for piano solo, from *Albumblätter*: Op. 124, No. 16]	Schumann

<Of the hero of the so called 'music of the future' I have found the following memoir.>

Wagner

was born at Leipsic in 1813. At an early age he began to write for the musical stage; and his reputation gradually increasing, he was appointed musical director of the Royal Theatre at Dresden, where several of his operas, particularly 'Rienzi,' 'Der fliegende Hollander,' 'Tannhäuser' and 'Lohengrin' were produced. Being of liberal principles, he became involved in the political troubles of Saxony in 1848, and was consequently formed [sic][1] into exile. He retired to Zurich where, we believe, he has ever since resided.

At the beginning of the year 1855 he accepted the invitation of the Philharmonic Society in London to undertake the conductorship of their concerts. He has contributed largely to the musical literature of the day, and his aesthetic opinions, as well as the merits of his operas, have become the subjects of a violent and wide-spread controversy; one party representing him as a real musical reformer and an artist of great and original genius whilst the other holds him to be a visionary in his notions, and extravagant and unintelligible in his taste.

The English public are not yet in a condition to form a just estimate of his character;[2] but in the meantime his dramatic pieces are more and more frequently performed at the principal theatres in Germany.

With regard to Wagner, I have no intention of [treating] him disrespectfully; that I entirely misunderstand him and his musical opinions may be my fault and not his. At any rate he possesses an influence at this moment over musical art, which it would be impossible to overlook.

My illustrations will conclude with a small example from his opera of Tannhäuser.

Duet, Pianoforte, from 'Tannhäuser'	Wagner

You will have noticed that my programme contains no specimen of English composition, and I trust that you will consider that I have

1 Doubtless a misreading of 'forced' on the part of Mary Bennett. It suggests that in this case she was copying from a rough draft of her husband's.

2 It was not until 1870 that the first staging of a Wagner opera took place in London: 'The Flying Dutchman', in Italian translation at Drury Lane Theatre.

exercised good taste in abstaining from setting up our countrymen in direct opposition to those whom I have brought to your notice this evening. Indeed I feel that the specimens which I have introduced of foreign musicians by no means do them full justice and must be taken only as a formal recognition of their merits and of the <important> position they hold in the world of art at the present moment. <Had it even been otherwise I should not have taken a different course, sensible that my duty this evening was more to draw your observation to the tendency of art-feeling in England than to make you believe we have art in all its strength and perfection.>[1]

[**Conclusion**]

<Bidding adieu to all my compliments as to home music> {But} I have now to say a very few words as to our chances as a musical nation in the future. There is no doubt [that] since the days of Purcell music in England has been advancing not by forced marches, but with that resolute step which betokens determination to perform the journey without the chance of a failure.

I always read with the greatest interest and the most intense jealousy a report of the proceedings of the Royal Academy of Arts in Trafalgar Square.[2] The title of this institution would seem to comprehend every branch of art.

Sir Joshua Reynolds, the first president of the Royal Academy, never failed to speak with the greatest respect for music, as inseparable from the sister arts, but whether his successors carry out his idea it seems problematical, since music is never invited to make its appearance within the walls of Trafalgar Square. To the Royal Academy of Arts government has ever given its unstinted aid.[3] It is true that we have a Royal Academy of Music, which <to be just> is most liberally <supported> {patronised} by Her Majesty and the royal family, but <as I have already hinted> our government does not contribute the smallest coin of the realm.[4]

1 This deleted sentence is written in a different hand, possibly Mary Bennett's.

2 Actually in Burlington House, Piccadilly.

3 This was evidently the final version of a passage that gave Bennett some trouble. A sentence deleted at the end of the previous paragraph reads: 'Referring you to my remarks, on the encouragement given by foreign governments <especially those of France and Belgium> to music, let me remind you that our own government never grants one sixpence to this department of the fine arts.' Another, pasted over, reads: 'I always read with the greatest interest and the most intense jealousy a report of the proceedings of the Royal Academy of Arts in Trafalgar Square [sic]; the title of this institution would seem to comprehend every branch of art.'

4 As a former student and instructor at the Royal Academy of Music (RAM), and as a pupil and friend of the recently retired principal, Cipriani Potter, Bennett no doubt had an

The musical Academy possesses a Royal Charter with the unenviable privilege of being allowed to sue and to be sued, but privileges connected with music none whatsoever. Contrast our means and the opportunities they present with those of France, Belgium, & Holland and the result will be any thing but creditable to Great Britain.

Nevertheless if music in England is forever to be the Cinderella of the fine arts, so like Cinderella of old, will she find her fairies ready to deck her with the gayest attire and to acknowledge her worth whilst her sisters are flaunting in high places? The fairies are the public, who watch over the interests of music and turn all Cinderella's mice into horses, her nutshells into carriages, and enable her eventually to ride over all obstacles that stand in the way.

With every respect for what Continental nations have done for musical art, to which this evening I have endeavoured to bear testimony, I come to the conclusion that England is better prepared than most nations to resist certain dangerous innovations, which, promoted by advocates more remarkable for eloquence than for love and knowledge of the art, threaten, even in Germany (for ages regarded as the stronghold of music), to subvert its principles and reduce it from its high position to that of a mere visionary paradox.

Our young musicians are travellers no longer content with the food which their parents bring them. They seek artistic nourishment for themselves, nor are they inclined to put up with pedlar's wares, no matter from what market imported. These and other signs encourage me in the belief that England, modest, laborious, and sincere in the pursuit of art, will ultimately (like Cinderella of the fairy tale already cited) in spite of all antagonistic influences be found worthy of the glass slipper.

intimate knowledge of its history and present financial straits. The first government grant to the RAM was not to be voted until 1864, when a paltry £500 per year was granted by the Gladstone administration, only to be withdrawn by Disraeli four years later (Scholes, *Mirror*, 694). By that time Bennett was himself principal of the RAM.

PART TWO

Lectures at the London Institution, 1864

On the Music for the Theatre Composed by Natives of Belgium, Italy, France, and Germany

5

[Dramatic Music]
[Early Forms of Opera]
On the Music for the Theatre by Belgian Composers

London Institution, 15 February 1864

Introduction

The original title of my lectures was as follows, 'The Dramatic Music of France, Belgium, Germany, and Italy.'

Having, somewhat hastily, adopted this high sounding title, I repented at leisure – a very little reflection reminded me that I had chosen a title far too comprehensive for the moderate intentions I had in view, and for the means of illustration at my disposal.

In taking the title 'Dramatic Music' I intended to speak only of that music written expressly for the theatre and of those composers who have been most prominent in the formation and development of the opera as it is now brought down to us.

Having made this admission, I am, at the same time, unwilling to spare myself altogether the consequences of my rashness, and shall endeavour to say a few words upon dramatic music in general – principally at the present moment, however, in regard to that music which strikes me as dramatic, apart from the stage; I mean that dramatic music to be found in the oratorio, in the sacred cantata, and that dramatic music which is to be found in the instrumental compositions of the great masters. As to that which is written for the stage, my lectures will sufficiently provide for, and I need not [in this Introduction], except incidentally, go into this branch, which, if not always dramatic in character, is always dramatic in name.

The term 'dramatic' as now used is, indeed, comprehensive and very difficult if not nearly impossible to define satisfactorily, in as much as the word itself is used to describe something indefinite. Nevertheless it is found to be a convenient term to describe any sensation out of the ordinary way caused by music upon the listener. It is nowadays used alike in relation to the oratorio, the opera, and the symphony. I am not prepared to deny that the rapid growth of music as an art, the heightened effects produced, combined with the sharpened appreciation of the audience, excuse a more general use of the word than it had a quarter of a century since – still it is often very heedlessly applied, and applied to compositions which from their tame and even character (however good in other respects) are incapable of arousing more than the ordinary sensation bestowed by pleasing music at all times and under all circumstances.

Some of our greatest men (be it reverently spoken) have been the least dramatic, when they must have wished to have been the most dramatic, and the contrary. There is much beautiful and grand music written for the stage, music of which I would have given my head to have written one bar, but which nevertheless gives me no idea of the dramatic, and which even improves when removed from the theatre to the concert room.

On the whole I am inclined to think that with the exception of the modern French composers (and here and there a rare exception in other schools), there is more real dramatic music (according to the idea I have of the title) written without reference to the stage, than that which is written expressly for it.

May I say, for instance, that I find more dramatic music in Beethoven's 'Mount of Olives' and even in his masses than in his opera of Fidelio. What can be found in 'Fidelio' equal in dramatic effect to the song in C minor[1] (Ex. 1)?

Ex. 1

with the magnificent recitative preceding it, only to be excelled by the powerfully touching recitatives of Seb. Bach in the 'Passions Music.'

Also, refer to the 'Qui tollis' in his Mass in C Minor[2] (Ex. 2), [and] again to the chorus of soldiers 'He came towards this mountain' (Ex. 3). These are wonderful evidences of Beethoven's dramatic genius, only

1 The examples in music notation must have been used as aide-mémoires when Bennett played the excerpts on the piano. The printed 'Programme of Illustrations' accompanying the lecture reads: 'Short Incidental Specimens from Beethoven's "Mount of Olives", Mass in C, Mendelssohn's "Hymn of Praise", Elijah. C. Minor Symphony — Beethoven.' Ex. 1 is the beginning of Jesus's aria 'Meine Seele ist erschüttert' from *Christus an Ölberge*.

2 Or rather C Major. The stave is blank except for the clef and signatures; it is filled in here with the appropriate music. In the margin, '3' is written opposite Ex. 2 and '2' opposite Ex. 3, indicating a change of order.

surpassed by those which are to be found in his instrumental works. Of these I shall speak very shortly.

Ex. 2

Ex. 3

Since writing my lecture[1] I find the following in regard to the 'Qui tollis' in Schindler's Life of Beethoven:

> In April 1823, the countess Shafgotsch brought him his first mass with a new German text, written by Mr Scholz, music director of Warmbrunn in Silesia. We were just at dinner. Beethoven quickly opened the manuscript and ran over a few pages. When he came to the qui tollis, the tears trickled down his cheeks and he was obliged to desist, saying with with the deepest emotion, in reference to the inexpressively beautiful text: 'Yes, that was precisely my feeling when I wrote this.' This, says Schindler, was the first and last time I saw him in tears.[2]

To go a little farther back, let us take the case of Handel. If one searches through the whole of his operas, there is scarcely a dramatic situation to be compared in feeling with that of the Trio between Solomon and the two mothers, 'Words are weak to paint my fears', which but for one slight blemish might rank with any thing which any musical dramatist has ever produced.[3]

Let us turn to Mendelssohn's sacred works (in spite of his beautiful music in the great plays, The Son & Stranger, Camacho, Lorelei &c). What has ever been done in the way of dramatic effect to surpass the 'Watchman will the night soon pass' (Ex. 4), gathering in intensity as it makes its way into the chorus 'The night is departing'?[4]

1 This paragraph is written on a facing page.

2 Bennett quoted this with only minor changes from Schindler, *Life of Beethoven*, 226–7.

3 A few blank lines follow. On a facing page Bennett wrote: 'Bach — Passion Musik — Haydn — (Creation) "And the Spirit of God" '.

4 From *Lobgesang*: the recitative following No. 6, at the words 'Hüter, ist die Nacht bald hin?'

Ex. 4

Watch- man, will the night soon pass?

But this is only one of the many glorious specimens which Mendelssohn has given of his dramatic power. Probably most of my audience are at this time wondering why I do not quote examples from 'St. Paul' & 'Elijah', and I only abstain from so doing having consideration to the time at my disposal, and from a conviction that these masterpieces are by this time thoroughly well known and appreciated by an English audience, although the first probably in a less degree than the second.

Upon second thoughts however, I will avail myself of one specimen from 'Elijah' as illustrating the very triumph of art – an effect which can never be heard without emotion, but which is the result of no straining or elaboration on the part of its composer; on the contrary, a gentle thought (not the less dramatic for that) having its birth in a mind of the highest cultivation.

Most of us, I think, know the chorus 'Behold, God the Lord passed by'[1] (Exx. 5, 6). What then can be more wonderful after all the passionate excitement of the first portion of this chorus than the modest, lovely ending (Ex. 7)?

Ex. 5
[Be - hold, God the Lord pas - sed by.]
Ex. 6
and a migh - ty wind
&c.
Ex. 7
And in that still voice. on- ward came the Lord

In giving these bright examples of Mendelssohn as a musical dramatist, let me exempt him, as indeed I do Cherubini and Spohr (the latter

1 'Der Herr ging vorüber'.

perhaps less heartily), from the charge of any want of dramatic power when writing for the stage. Had I really this very weak intention, the music in 'The Midsummer Night's Dream' would rise up against me, although be it remembered that the overture upon which the music is based was written many years before, and as a concert-room piece. In fact, the object of all the remarks I have made up to this moment is not to prove the scarcity of dramatic music for the theatre but only to show the abundance of purely dramatic music which does not receive any support from scenic effect or stage accessories.

Instrumental Dramatic Music

We come now to another department of the art, where pure instances of the dramatic power and effect are by no means rare – where Beethoven commands, and where Mozart is entirely at his ease – where Mendelssohn revels, and where Weber (strange to say) performs the part of the passionate lover (taking his great sonatas and excepting his theatrical overtures, which is a fair proceeding) rather than the magician one would expect to find him.

This is the branch of the art which justifies the compliment Goethe has paid to it: 'The worth of art appears most eminent in music. Since it requires no material, no subject matter, whose effect must be deducted: it is wholly form and power, and raises and ennobles whatever it expresses.'[1]

A much smaller though most useful man (Dr Burney) has written: 'Music, considered abstractedly, without the assistance (or rather shackles) of speech, and abandoned to its own powers, is now become a rich, expressive, and picturesque language in itself: having its forms, proportions, contrasts, punctuations, phrases and periods.'[2]

Now many persons have the idea that every piece of music is intended to describe something – that a composer has always something before him, which he is shaping into musical form. Such a question as the following is often asked: 'I wonder what Beethoven had in his mind when he wrote this sonata.'

Now we are told by Beethoven himself what he had in his mind when he wrote the Pastorale Symphony,[3] and we are also told by more characteristics than the Funeral March what was the idea which prompted the 'Eroica' Symphony. But has any body ever been told or has any body ever

1 See Goethe, *Maximen und Reflexionen*, 1239. Bennett's source for the English text is not known; he may have translated it himself.

2 Burney, *General History*, 2:171 (1935 ed., 2:511). Burney wrote '. . . forms, proportions, contrasts, punctuations, *members*, phrases, and periods' [italics added].

3 Bennett is referring to the brief programme note that Beethoven attached to the score.

found out what was the feeling which gave rise to the composition of the C Minor Symphony? Yet in the whole range of music there can be found nothing more thoroughly dramatic, more entrancing, more heart-stirring than this noble creation. Some of the points indeed place the listener beyond the control of his own feelings.

Take the following example, being the re-introduction of the Scherzo into the march (Ex. 8).

Ex. 8

I could easily take up the whole evening in bringing forward similar beautiful cases (see the Choral Symphony) but as it is my duty to do justice to other authors besides Beethoven, I must move onward, not forgetting on my way the claims of J. Seb. Bach and Mozart as great dramatists in instrumental composition. The prelude of Bach which you shall hear I take to be a lovely bit of dramatic music, and the fantasia of Mozart will do more to describe to you what really is dramatic music than all I have been saying up to this moment. {As another specimen, you will also hear one of the Lieder of Mendelssohn.}[1]

[1] This example is preceded by two blank staves headed 'Prelude E. minor Organ Fugue'.

Ex. 9

I must now leave (and not without regret) this portion of my subject, which I have dealt upon at some length, in consideration of the explanation which was due to you on the alteration of the title of my lectures.[1]

I have still to set myself right upon another point, and that is, as to the order of my lectures – this will not be quite so deep an affair as the accidental expression of dramatic music, so I will explain myself at once, feeling sure that the alteration in my plan will be of no consequence whatever to my audience.

The long introduction which I have made this evening (and which is not yet over) could not have come before any of these lectures where much operatic music has to be spoken of, as will be the case in the lectures on Italian, French and German composers. I thought it therefore would be more convenient to you and to myself to take the music of the only Belgian operatic composers I can find, this evening.

Another plan which I shall adopt is to speak of composers under the countries in which they were born – and in this way I reclaim Grétry from France and restore him to Belgium, where you shall hear some of his excellent music. In like manner, Lulli will go back to Italy after a long life in France. There exists great confusion in the present day as to the nationalities and characteristics of composers. Meyerbeer produces all his great works on the French stage, but he is not a French composer. Handel wrote most of his Italian operas in England and for the Haymarket, but he is a German, and wrote several operas before he left his native country. Cherubini was five and twenty when he left his native country to take up Paris as his adopted home. Gluck confesses without hesitation that his latest and best operas were modelled according to the English taste which he had carefully studied on his visit to England; but his music is no more English than Purcell's is German. Many composers who might be classed with Purcell, Handel and Gluck in their day are now forgotten, while these three men are coming closer to us. A new

There is no way to know which of Bach's E-minor organ preludes was played. The Mendelssohn *Lied ohne Worte*, according to the *Musical World* report (vol. 42 (1864), 121), was Book 5, No. 5, in A minor.

1 This refers to the change from 'The Dramatic Music of France, Belgium, Germany and Italy' (referred to at the beginning of this lecture) to the one on the printed syllabus, 'The Music for the Theatre Composed by Natives of Belgium, Italy, France, and Germany'. It seems that Bennett had decided on, or agreed to, the change of title without making a corresponding change in the content of the present lecture, the first half of which still deals with non-theatre music.

arrangement of all these matters is extremely desirable. It is high time that we should be able to speak of Handel as an operatic writer without being obliged to speak of Bononcini as his rival. At one time Mozart could scarcely be spoken of without being bracketed with Pleyel or Salieri.

I go now to the 'early form of opera.'

Early Form of Opera

It is universally agreed that we are indebted to Italy for the opera form.

Its invention is even more closely traced than to ascribe it to a mere country – it is traced even to a city; nay even to a private house. Historians of music are unanimous in their writings upon this subject.

To Florence, then, are we indebted for this important step in the art – and to the enthusiasm of a few professors and amateurs, who in the 16th century united themselves with the sole and direct object of elevating music, and art generally.

The house of Count Vernio[1] at Florence was the rendezvous of these benefactors. Among the party are to be found the names of Jacopo Peri, Giulio Caccini, Galilei, and Emilio Cavaliere, names which should be remembered with gratitude as long as music exists.

It would take a long space of time to describe the gradual birth of the stage opera, arising out of the sacred drama, but this has been done over and over again, and can be studied by those more than usually interested in the subject through the works of Burney, Hawkins, Fétis, Kiesewetter, Hogarth and others. I must, however, as a matter of great interest, dwell for a few moments upon the merits of the Florentine dilettante before mentioned.

We find in Burney a quotation from one, whom he calls a learned, an elegant writer, on music (Giovanni Battista Doni): a curious and instructive account of the first operas which were performed at Florence.

This writer says – 'Some kind of Cantilena, or melody, has been introduced at all times, either in the form of interludes between the acts: or occasionally, in the body and business of the piece. But it is still fresh in the memory of every one, at what period the whole drama was set to music and sung from the beginning to the end, because anterior to the attempt of Emilio Cavaliere there seems to have been nothing of the kind worth mention. This composer published a drama at Rome in 1600 called "Dell' Animo e del Corpo." It will be necessary' (proceeds the

[1] Giovanni de' Bardi, Count of Vernio, host of the Camerata and patron of the inventors of monody which was the distinctive ingredient of early opera. Today he is more often called Count Bardi.

quotation) 'to declare here, that the melodies in this work are very different from such as are at present composed in what is commonly called recitative; being no other than ariets, full of contrivance, repetition, echoes, &c, which are totally different from the true and genuine theatrical music, of which Signor Emilio could know nothing, from want of being acquainted with ancient authors and the usages of antiquity. It may therefore be said, that the first attempt at reviving theatrical music after having been lost for so many ages was made at Florence, where so many noble arts have been recovered.'[1]

The same writer speaks of Count Vernio and the meetings at his house. He says, 'There resided in that city (Florence) during these times Signor Conti di Vernio, who was afterwards called to the service of Pope Clement the 8th by whom he was most tenderly beloved and made maestro di camera. This most accomplished nobleman was particularly attached to the study of antiquity and to the theory and practice of music, to which he had applied himself for so many years so closely that he became, for the time in which he lived, a correct and good composer. His house was the constant rendezvous of all persons of genius, and a kind of flourishing academy, where the young nobility often assembled to pass their hours of leisure in laudable exercises and learned discourse, but particularly on musical subjects, it being the wish of all the company to recover that art of which the ancients related such wonders.

'During these discussions, it was universally allowed that as modern (?) music was extremely deficient in grace, and in the expression of words, it became necessary that some other species of cantilena or melody should be tried, by which the words should not be rendered unintelligible, nor the verse destroyed.'[2]

This then (to drop quotation) describes the dawning of a new state of things for the opera, and such as was initiated, developed and carried out by the party at Count Vernio's house. And what a delightful party it must have been!

Who of us here present, but would have been delighted to have been one of this society – to have heard the notions for the improvement of music propounded by Galilei, to have heard the animated performance of Giulio Caccini Romano, who is described as a young, elegant and spirited singer, composing and singing to a single instrument, which was generally the theorbo or large lute? With what regret must this party have witnessed the departure of the genial accomplished Count Vernio from Florence. But it is related that Signor Jacopo Corsi took his place

1 Burney, *General History* (1935 ed.), 2, 511–12, translating a passag from G. B. Doni, *Opera omnia* II (Florence, 1763).
2 Burney, *General History* (1935 ed.), 2, 512.

and became the patron of music, as of every other art and science, and that his house continued to be the retreat of the muses.

It was this Jacopo Corsi who supplied the text to the first new form of operatic composition, the result of all the meditations at Count Vernio's house. The name of the work was 'Dafne'; it was set to music by Peri and was followed by other similar works, increasing gradually in importance and in the favour of the public.[1]

I have now brought the history of opera down to about that point at which we shall meet it on Monday next, and so for this evening I leave it.

Music of Belgium

I come now to the musicians of Belgium, and although they have not provided us with much variety in the way of music for the theatre, I cannot commence with their doings in this respect without calling your attention to their earnest work in the cause of music generally, which they and all the musicians of the Low Countries have persevered in from the 14th century to the present time.

We read of them going abroad in large numbers, not only to Italy, but to Spain, Germany, and France, composing, teaching and directing choirs, never weary in their endeavours to disseminate music, and although they themselves have not produced any thing in abundance for the theatre, it is not improbable that the Italians (of whom I shall speak next Monday) have reason to be grateful to the musicians of the Low Countries for what they do in this department of the art.

But yet, if the Low Countries cannot produce you many composers of stage music, they can, and do, point to one Belgian musician as an operatic writer of the first water. This composer is Grétry. Although known principally by his connection with the French school, it will be found hereafter that his music is thoroughly individual and belongs no more to France than it does to Italy.

I will not detain you with much of the personal history of Grétry, which however is by no means devoid of interest. I will just mention that he was born at Liège in the year 1741 and died in the year 1813. He appears to have had the advantage of a first rate musical education, commencing it in his native town, then pursuing it for eight or nine years in Rome, and finally working out his experience in Paris. It is said that he composed 55 operas between the years 1765 and 1803.

Two of Grétry's operas are known to the English stage, Zémire et Azor and Richard Cœur de Lion. They were produced in an English form some years since and made Grétry's name very popular.[2]

[1] Of course, these events were not open to the 'public' in the broader sense.

[2] *Richard Coeur de Lion* had its first English production in 1786, *Zémire et Azor* in 1776.

I have chosen one piece from each of three operas by Grétry. They are very distinct in character, and, I believe, good specimens of his style, which is at once simple, elegant and expressive, and when necessary, not without vivacity.

The first specimen is an air from the opera of 'Azor et Zémire' – this will be found sombre and pathetic in character.

Air, 'Le pauvre enfant ne savait pas' (Zémire et Azor)	Grétry

A second example is from the opera of 'Richard Cœur de Lion' – an animated, martial piece of music.

Air, 'Si l'univers entire m'oublie' (Richard Cœur de Lion)	Grétry

As a proof of Grétry's variety of style, I have selected an air from the comic opera of 'Le tableau parlant'. The general character of this song is light and simple and is ingeniously relieved by a middle portion in the minor key.

Air, 'Vous étiez ce que vous n'êtes plus' (Le tableau parlant)	Grétry

The reappearance of Grétry's works in the music warehouses of the present, published in neat and fashionable form, sufficiently proves that it is music with which the public cannot afford to dispense.[1] In fact, it is music which, when even compared with larger works, continues to give pleasure. Young composers might with advantage copy Grétry in many respects, while they might with equal advantage avoid many errors in the ultra modern school. It is much to the credit of Berlioz, a French musician, that he insists upon this point, and has written a pamphlet on the subject.[2]

With regard to modern Belgian operatic writers, I regret that I can do little more than mention these names, not having been able to procure specimens which would answer my purpose.

Fétis, the eminent writer, has composed several operas which have obtained average success. One of these has, I believe, been performed in England.[3]

1 It is possible that Bennett is referring here to Adolphe Adam's free arrangements of *Richard Coeur de Lion* and *Zémire et Azor*. I am grateful to Katharine Ellis for this suggestion.

2 An article by Berlioz, 'Quelques mots sur les anciens compositeurs, et sur Grétry en particulier' (*Revue et gazette musicale* 4/6 (5 February 1837), 45–6), championed the older French composers but did not specifically recommend them as models. No 'pamphlet' on the subject is known to exist. I am grateful to Hugh Macdonald for information on this point.

3 Fétis's comic opera *La vieille* (1826) had indeed appeared in two English-language

Hanssens, born at Ghent in 1802, is another composer of music for the theatre, held in the highest estimation in Belgium.

But just at the last moment, I have made the acquaintance of an opera ('Georgette' by Gevaert) which has enchanted me and gives me great hope that a Belgian Gounod may have arrived. I regret that, procuring the work so recently, I can do nothing more than play you one little romance in it – but this a choice specimen.

Romance in G Minor (Georgette)	Gevaert

Gevaert was born at Ghent in the year 1829. We should have known more of him by this time, but as in the case of Gounod, this talent did not appeal even to himself, until he had long been employed (and not unsuccessfully) in the composition of music in other styles. The opera (from which I have just played an extract) was composed in 1852 and met with extreme success.[1]

In conclusion, let me promise that if I have not on the present occasion been able to do entire justice to the efforts of Belgian operatic composers, I will not forget to make ample amends in the future.

If they are not <u>numerically</u> strong, they have in <u>quality</u> done much for the music of the theatre, and as musicians <u>in general</u> they are worthy of our highest esteem. I have often thought to myself, that if I could not be a German musician, then I should like to be a Belgian musician. My idea is, that if any new school of opera music should arise, it will come from Belgium and compete with France in <u>individuality</u>.

The Belgians have an earnest and clear conscience in what they are doing. They have the enfolding arm of government (a thing unknown in England). They have an academy, which admits without distinction and almost without payment all young students who choose to avail themselves of its great advantages.

All power to Belgium – to the king, and to the government, who thus set an example to the rest of the world in the encouragement of musical art. Belgium has sent out the finest performers in all classes, performers not to be surpassed by those of any other nation.

Once more, should a bright dramatic era dawn upon Belgium, it will not be more welcome than deserved.

adaptations: *Love in Wrinkles; or, The Russian Stratagem*, adapted by Michael Rophino Lacy (Drury Lane, 1828) and *My Old Woman*, adapted by George Macfarren, senior (Surrey Theatre, 1829).

[1] *Georgette, ou Le moulin de Fontenoy* was premiered at Paris in 1853. A piano-vocal score was published at Brussels in 1854. No. 2 is a Romance, 'Que j'ai presque envie de pleurer'. Loewenberg lists no performance in England of this or any other opera by Gevaert.

6

On the Music for the Theatre Composed by Natives of Italy

London Institution, 22 February 1864

I will ask you, in reference to my lecture of last Monday, in which I gave a sketch of my plan and arrangement, including a short account of the early opera down to the time it took a definite form, to remember that when I speak of Italian composers for the theatre, I do not undertake to connect them with that which is now called 'the Italian opera'; nor do I undertake any thing like a continuous history of the opera or lyric drama of Italy or of any other country beyond that which may arise out of the order in which I mention the composers brought forward and the specimens exhibited. Under the classification I have adopted it will be difficult to keep long with the so-called Italian opera.[1]

It is true that for some long time after the production of the first opera 'Dafne' at Florence, Italy was the lyric stage and Italians were the composers, but this state of things could not last for an indefinite period, and we accordingly find after the lapse of a reasonable time that authors, composers and performers of other countries lend their aid to that form of lyric drama imitated at Florence.

In later times we know how Handel, Gluck and Mozart worked for the opera. Gluck (whose name will come more prominently before you under the list of German composers of the theatre) is acknowledged to have been one of the greatest benefactors to this branch of the musical art.

Indeed it seems that at the present time the Italians are passing over the responsibility and care of the Italian opera to composers and performers of other countries, and that they have no longer the strength, energy and means to support it. We have only to look at our daily

1 Here Bennett is evidently struggling with the consequences of his decision to classify national schools of opera according to the country of birth of the composers concerned.

advertisements to find French & German composers invading the Italian stage, and more than this we find that many of the principal singers are German, Swedish & Hungarian. I have heard a recent case quoted where the opera performed was composed by a German, and where not a single Italian took a principal part.

While lamenting the interrupted succession of the beautiful singers we have been accustomed to welcome from Italy, we should on the other hand feel grateful that we are so admirably supplied from other sources; and that our own country is able to perform so honorable a part in the aid of vocal performance.

Being upon this point, I will for a moment enter on an enquiry of some little interest. Are Italian singers disappearing because Italian composers are absenting themselves? or are Italian composers losing heart because they can find no more Pastas or Grisis? At any rate they are much dependent upon each other, and the simultaneous retirement of both is a point worthy of remark.

The list of composers set down for this evening seems at first sight somewhat scanty.

I could without any trouble have increased the number of composers four times, and the number of specimens to almost any amount, but I could not have increased the number of distinctive marks which the specimens I have chosen exhibit.

Many composers who in their day could be distinguished from each other appear, when viewed from a distance of time and tested by principles of improved art, identical, and are but faint imitations of some particular man at the head of their era. These mere imitations soon disappear, never to return. History has no room for duplicates, and it is only the composer who has done something for himself, who has written his name, nay, even his initials on <the> art [that] can expect to be quoted whenever the art is mentioned. Such men have I chosen this evening, to illustrate the progress of the lyric drama as supported by pure Italians. It is very possible that I have not been strictly just in my selection, but at any rate I have tried to be so.

Again, of course we acknowledge degrees of genius and individuality in any number of men when classed together; and there are some two or three men in the list of this evening far beyond the others classed with them, and although I shall in the course of my lecture hope to speak of them at greater length, and through their works do them greater justice than through my words, I cannot refrain from pointing out to you at once before we proceed to illustration such names as Alessandro Scarlatti, Cherubini, and Rossini. These are names which always preserve Italy from the sneers of those who see her <decadence> {decay} in operatic art with something akin to pleasure.

Lulli

The name which should be the first on my list[1] is accidentally omitted, and I must supply it: I mean the name of the celebrated Lully, born in 1634. It is the more necessary that I should do so, as by my classification Lulli is taken away from the French composers of opera under which class he is more generally known and placed with those of his own countrymen. The artistic and personal life of Lulli is of great interest. He left his native country at the age of ten years, and ultimately became one of the greatest benefactors to the French opera.

I have this morning transcribed two short specimens from his opera of 'Roland' which I will play to you, although they do him but feeble justice.

Two excerpts from Roland	Lully

[Carissimi]

To begin[2] with Carissimi. Although he appears to have written no operas, still he contributed greatly to the cultivation of operatic music, as far as its form is concerned. I did not despair, until the last moment, of finding some specimen of his works for the theatre, but I have failed, and therefore that he may not be entirely without a link between himself and his celebrated pupil, Alessandro Scarlatti, I will play a few bars from a cantata entitled 'Mary Queen of Scots' which I have found in Burney.[3]

Ex. 10

'The praises lavished on Carissimi by his contemporaries were inexhaustible, and they seemed to consider that through his means, an approach had been made to the golden age of the art.'[4] Perhaps the

1 The printed 'Programme of Illustrations' accompanying the lecture.

2 This shows that the preceding section on Lully, including the illustrations, was added as an afterthought.

3 This is an inaccurate version of the opening phrase of the aria 'A morire', omitting the last note (C), evidently copied from Burney, *General History*, 2: 69. The complete cantata, *Ferma, lascia ch'io parti (Il lamento di Maria di Scozia)*, may be found in Massenkeil, *Cantatas*, 132.

4 From Kiesewetter, *History of the Modern Music*, 203–4. The underlining of 'his' is Bennett's.

soundest proof of the greatness of Carissimi was the attracting to him, as a pupil, [of] young Alessandro Scarlatti, who, it is said, 'burned with intense desire to render himself perfect, as a composer, under the guidance of so distinguished a master.'[1] Scarlatti must have known and understood enough of Carissimi not to be mistaken in his choice.

[Alessandro Scarlatti]

Alessandro Scarlatti, who is described as the link which united the new music to that of ancient times – also described as the forerunner of the beautiful period of Italian music, in contradistinction to the grand period from Palestrina to the Neapolitan School – was born at Naples in the year 1659. He is spoken of as great in almost every department of the art, using his powerful influence in preparing the way to that eminence which music subsequently attained.

Among other accomplishments, he is said to have been a great performer on the harp, by means of which he first introduced himself to Carissimi. Although there are many of his cantatas extant, his operas (about one hundred in number) together with several oratorios and masses are all lost.[2]

I regret, therefore, that I can give you no specimen of his music for the theatre – but I could not have passed over the name of Alessandro Scarlatti without this slight tribute to his greatness, and to his exertions for this department in music. Alessandro Scarlatti died in 1728, having survived to witness the glory of many of his own pupils.

His son, Domenico, is well known through his works for the harpsichord. In the volume of harpsichord lessons published by Walsh will be found a fugue (in F minor) which I have always heard attributed to his father Alessandro, by what authority I cannot say. I only know that it is a very fine fugue.[3]

[Stradella]

Stradella of Naples[4] was born in 1650, a fine composer of the church and theatre, also a great performer on the violin. Among his operas we find

1 It is not impossible that Scarlatti was a pupil of Carissimi, but the latter died when Scarlatti was only 13.

2 A large number have, of course, been found since Bennett's time.

3 The only F-minor example in the *Essercizi per gravicembalo* by Domenico Scarlatti published by Walsh of London in 1738/9 is No. 19 (K. 19), which is no fugue. The only fugue is No. 30 in G minor, sometimes called 'The Cat's Fugue' (K. 30). There is no reason to think either was composed by his father.

4 This and several subsequent pages and sections have years at their head ('1689', etc.). As these are often inaccurate and have little significance they have been omitted.

one entitled 'La forza dell' amor'. The specimen chosen conveys a good idea of the serious, earnest tone for which this musician was celebrated.

Air (La forza del amor paterno)[1]	Stradella

[Jommelli]

Jommelli was born in 1714 at Aversa, near Naples. He composed his first opera 'L'errore amorosa' at the age of twenty three. After having written many beautiful and successful works of this class, it is said that the failure of his last opera[2] (through a bad performance) affected him so deeply that he became paralyzed. Jommelli died in the [year] 1774. With him, I might have associated Pergolesi, who is described as 'the child of taste and elegance', but my time does not permit me to increase my specimens of the art, as it stood at this period.

Air, 'Pensa che figlio' [(Attilio regolo)]	Jommelli

Sacchini & Sarti

I have bracketed these elegant composers together, they having lived in the same time, and performed about an equal share in the progress of the Italian lyric drama.

Both the specimens I bring forward are in the shape of vocal trios from their celebrated operas. The one of Sarti's is especially beautiful, and worthy of any composer.

Trio, 'O lieto di'[3]	Sacchini
Trio, 'Che vi par, [Dorina bella]' [(*I rivali delusi*)]	Sarti

Cimarosa

Cimarosa was born at Naples in the year 1754. The life of Cimarosa is so well drawn in Hogarth's History of Music, that I will make no apology for making a quotation from it.[4]

1 Almost certainly this was the aria 'Cosí Amor mi fai languir', since it was the only aria from this opera then in print, in Enrico Rung, *Musica scelta de' antichi maestri italiani* (Copenhagen, [1855]). See Gianturco and McCrickard, *Alessandro Stradella*.

2 This probably refers to the bungled production of *Ifigenia in Tauride* at Naples in 1771.

3 An Italian version of 'O doux moment' from *Œdipe à Colone*.

4 The reference 'Hogarth 193' is given at the end of the paragraph. Presumably Bennett read directly from Hogarth's book at this point. A likely excerpt from p. 193 has been supplied here.

[Domenico Cimarosa was born at Naples in 1754. . . His reputation as a dramatic composer spread with great rapidity, and was supported by a succession of works, which he continued to produce down to the period of his death, which took place at Venice in 1801. . . His masterpiece, Il matrimonio segreto, was brought out at Vienna in 1792, and received with an admiration which remains unabated even at this day. The emperor, who was present at the first representation of this opera, was so transported with it, that he invited the whole [of the] performers to a banquet, and sent them back the same evening to the theatre, where they played it a second time.

When Naples was possessed by the French, Cimarosa imbibed the revolutionary spirit of the time, and made himself so conspicuous for his political opinions, that he was thrown into prison, and it is said that his death was occasioned by the severity of the treatment he received. On his liberation in 1800, he went to Venice, where he brought out his opera, L'imprudente fortunata; and had composed an act of another piece, L'Artemisia, when his progress was arrested by death: it was completed by some other composer, and brought out on the stage at Venice. . .

Cimarosa was a man of highly cultivated mind, and an amiable disposition. His reply to a painter, who wished to pay him a compliment by saying he was superior to Mozart, exhibited wit as well as modesty:— 'I superior to Mozart, sir! —what would you say to any man who should tell you that you were superior to Raphael?']

Aria, 'Pria che spunti' [(Il matrimonio segreto)]	Cimarosa

Cherubini

Cherubini is a composer who must command the highest admiration of all who love music. He has made his mark upon the art. He is equally great in the church, the theatre, or the concert room. A celebrated modern critic observes that Cherubini's style may be called the mixed style, scientific enough to have received its education in Vienna, but yet tinged by the more melodious qualities which adorn the compositions of equally favored natives of Italy.

There is no doubt that this great man will be remembered when most Italians are forgotten. He will, like many another musician, suffer from the periodical inconstancy of the musical public, but will as often reappear. His music has in it the vitality of centuries.

Aria from Lodoiska	Cherubini

Spontini

Spontini was born at Jesi, in the Roman States, in 1778. His most celebrated operas are the 'Vestale' & 'Fernando Cortez'. I regret that I have no time to give a long history of Spontini, and indeed that I have done so little justice in this respect to all those composers I have mentioned – but their works will help them more than I can.

The duett which you will now hear is a splendid specimen of Spontini's manner.

Duetto, 'Quando amistà'[1] (La Vestale)	Spontini

Rossini

We come now to a composer who demands more than a passing remark – we come to one who has influenced the lyric Italian drama even more than his great predecessor Alessandro Scarlatti.

Rossini (who, if spared until next Monday, will have completed his 72nd year, and who was already busy in the art more than fifty years since), has taken the most extraordinary share in the existence and diffusion of operatic music. Upon no other man has such a variety of criticism been expended.

As to the actual place he should already enjoy in the history of art and its progress, it is not fully agreed; still less can it be foretold what position future historians may assign him when writing of his doings, and comparing him with musicians of his time. Still it is not difficult to pronounce him, at once, one of the most [gifted?] geniuses the world has ever produced.

When I say that the <critics> {opinions} of the present day have not decided upon the position Rossini should enjoy, I enter at once into a point of great interest – I mean that charge which has been so often brought against him of having introduced a false model of opera, and having set an example to young composers of his day in the total neglect of grammatical rules and the introduction of noisy instrumentation.

The first symptoms of decay in the operatic music of the Italians have been by some dated from the appearance of Rossini. All the faults of those who came after him are laid at his door, but it has been well said in speaking of his imitators, that they are 'much more successful in copying his defects than his beauties. They are, like him, full of mannerism: with this difference, that his manner was his own, while theirs is his.'[2]

Rossini's idea of dramatic treatment is perhaps not always consistent, as for example the trifling subject of the overture to the tragic opera of Semiramide & other cases.[3]

1 An Italian version of 'Quand l'amitié seconde mon courage'.

2 A quotation from Hogarth's *History of Music*, which Bennett had also used in Lecture 1 (p. 35).

3 A blank stave follows in the manuscript. Here the 'subject' of the overture to *Semiramide* has been supplied by the editor.

Ex. 11

But these are mere specks on his reputation as a great musical dramatist.

The longer Rossini lives, the more his reputation increases – <by some>. Without writing any more he gains immensely by the constant comparisons made between him and his successors. His loss to the Italian lyric drama is much greater than was at first supposed.

I give a short but lovely specimen of Rossini's music.

Aria, 'Assisa [a' piè d'un salice]' (Otello)	Rossini

Conclusion

Having now exhausted my programme of specimens from great Italian composers for the theatre, I must be allowed to say a few words as to the future of Italy in regard to the lyric drama.

I have not given you any examples of modern works later than those of Rossini, because such examples are within your easy reach, and because, in my opinion, which I give with great hesitation, they do not point to any probable improvement in the art arising from their existence.

The operas of Bellini, Donizetti, & Verdi have long been known and admired for their beautiful melodies, and in many cases, great dramatic situations – but they lack much that should allow them to endure. The so-called 'cantilena' of the Italian opera has now become tiresome from its extreme languor, unrelieved as it is by any grand finales or concerted music, never overlooked by the purely great masters.

How much would we give to hear from any of Rossini's successors such a 'finale' as that to the first act of the 'Barbiere'! And yet he is pointed to as the vicious model. But as I have already spoken at length upon Rossini, I need not once more attempt to defend him.

A much deeper reason for the decay of the lyric drama of Italy must be found than pointing to a doubtful model, doubtfully imitated. It may be also observed that the decline of the opera in Italy was prophesied long before Rossini was born.

There will always be a fashion in art to a great extent, and this will be more especially prevalent in the Italian opera, an entertainment almost exclusively provided for and maintained by the higher classes.

The composers of this branch of entertainment (I still speak of the Italians) know too little of the world – they are too much petted and caressed in a small coterie to <gain> {retain} that strength of form and outline which a rough acquaintance with the larger world gives to those who are not afraid to experience its wholesome lessons. Again, when the immediate fondness for their works subsides, they have no other branch of the art to fall back upon to keep their names in the constant recollection of the public.

Step by step has weakness overtaken the composers of music for the theatre in Italy. Bit by bit are they yielding their ancient proud position, until at last their almost final extinction is by many proclaimed. But should the oft-repeated proverb in their case be verified that 'Wherever an art has fallen, the blame must rest with the artists',[1] there are many friends of Italian music who would deplore this state of things.

The Italian composers have still that intuitive feeling for melody of which, it seems, no fate can deprive them; they have enriched their works with greater variety of harmony and musical coloring than can be found in the works of their predecessors, but they are fast losing form and outline, and the <necessary> elaboration indispensable in works destined to become permanent.

Still I cannot leave them, in gratitude for their past doings, without a hope {in which you will all join me} that their period of extinction as composers of the theatre is yet remote.

1 The source of this 'proverb' has not been found.

7

On the Music for the Theatre Composed by Natives of France

London Institution, 7 March 1864

A country which can include in its list of composers for the theatre the names of Rameau, Méhul, Auber, Hérold, Boieldieu, Halévy, Berlioz, with many others scarcely less eminent, can bear favorable comparison with any other nation where the art is cultivated and enjoyed. Had J. J. Rousseau lived to witness the complete development of the French school of lyric music, he might probably have rewritten his celebrated letter of 1753,[1] substituting praise for censure.

You will observe that I have, in my list of this evening, drawn lines of separation, firstly between Rameau and Méhul, and again between Méhul and Boieldieu. I will endeavour to explain why I have done this.

Rameau stands alone as a native French composer of opera of the epoch in which he lived. His predecessor was Lulli the Italian, and his successor was the famous Grétry the Belgian, both of whom I have already brought before you in my former lectures. Had I been giving a history of the lyric drama itself, these names must have been bracketed together, but tonight Rameau stands alone, there being, as far as I know, no native composer of his time worthy to be classed with him.

Again, the name of Méhul should on every account be as far removed from Rameau as those who come after Méhul should be separated from him. It is not only in consideration of the immense advance in the art which the compositions of Méhul exhibit, when comparing them with those of his compatriot Rameau, that this line of separation is rendered necessary; but it must also be admitted that the absence of one illustrious name immediately previous to Méhul creates a gap which it would not be wise to pass over without some explanation.

[1] The *Lettre sur la musique française*, published at Paris in 1753, in which Rousseau compared French music unfavourably with Italian.

One must not suppose that the French lyric drama passed over at once from Rameau on to the shoulders of Méhul. The great master of the situation at this moment was Gluck, and Méhul was his disciple. I must not be tempted to speak of Gluck the German (except thus incidentally) this evening; he will take a most honorable place in my lecture on 'The Music by Composers Native of Germany'. I have been obliged just to name him, in introducing his illustrious pupil.

After Méhul commences that exciting period in the history of French opera music, which continues down to our time. Boieldieu, Auber and Hérold (the second still alive to grace the art with his presence) must have the credit of inaugurating this new life in the French lyric drama.

Boieldieu, Auber, & Hérold are in the French operatic music what Alessandro Scarlatti was in the Italian, and Gluck in the German. They are creators, and have inspired their followers. While other schools have been declining and losing all distinguishing characteristics, the French opera composers have been rearing their own temple.

It seems to me that nothing in art of the present day can compare in freshness and completeness with the modern French opera from the time of Boieldieu, Auber and Hérold. The French opera composers have thrown off the leading strings of those great masters who previously helped them. They are not even to be influenced by such illustrious visitors as Rossini, Meyerbeer, and hosts of others – composers, singers, and performers – constantly in Paris.[1] If any nation may be said to make its own music, it is France. But perhaps this individuality has its drawback.

In England we know comparatively little of French opera music; but what has been presented to us has rarely met with any thing but great success. The 'Masaniello' of Auber has been brought on our stage, first as a grand ballet, where, contrary to stage practice {in pantomimic art}, the prayer scene in the market place was sung and made a remarkable impression;[2] subsequently this great work was produced as an opera in an English dress, and since then has been often played in England on the Italian stage.

Auber's 'Gustave' is also a work well known to opera visitants of a few years back. 'The Crown Diamonds' [*Les diamants de la couronne*] is another work which has endeared itself to the English public; but especially have we been fond of the opera 'Fra diavolo.'

The overtures or instrumental introductions to these French operas are thoroughly well known and enjoyed – for instance 'Zampa' and 'Le pré aux clercs' of Hérold, 'La dame blanche' of Boieldieu, &c, &c. But

1 On a facing page opposite this paragraph Bennett wrote in pencil: 'To be improved'.

2 A ballet based on Auber's *La Muette de Portici* was performed for the first time at the King's Theatre on 24 March 1829.

compared with what we know of the operas of German and Italian composers our acquaintance with the lyric drama by French composers is slight.

There are doubtless many substantial reasons why the modern French opera is not oftener brought on our boards; among the principal of which, must be reckoned the necessity of having singers who will thoroughly identify themselves with the characteristics of the music – who will really *pro tem.* become French singers, and leave their Italian manner behind them. Music so individual must have individual treatment.

Again, it is not one or two good singers or actors alone who can (as is too often the case with modern Italian operas) carry a French opera through successfully, for much to the honour of the French composers for the theatre, their operas are so completely constructed and so industriously elaborated, notwithstanding the brilliancy and spontaneity of the themes, that nothing but a finished performance in all the details can do them justice before the public.[1]

But there may be still a deeper and wider reason why we don't know more of the pure French opera. Is it, that as much as we admire the beautiful things the French composers create, they make no absolute impression upon us? They dash before us; we admire their sparkle, hoping it may return, but not caring to run after it. I confess, in sincerity, that this is much the feeling which I have toward French music; and I believe that this is about the feeling entertained by other musical nations toward the truly musical nation of France. When I hear the beautiful French music, it puts me in about the same frame [of] mind which I find myself in when looking into a shop window filled with the choicest and most brilliant articles, none of which I intend to purchase, and the possession of which does not for a moment excite my envy.

It is clear that with all the individuality of the music of the French opera school, all young musicians of other countries are not excited to imitate it. They prefer, whether wisely or not, to engraft their ideas upon other models, and they either become languid Italians or mysterious Germans.

Having made this rather long introduction, I must ask to go at once to my programme of illustrations and speak briefly of the French masters whose names I have selected to uphold the honour of the richly merited reputation of their country.

[1] A paragraph written on the facing page reads: 'It is to the superiority of its national theatre that France owes that of its lyric drama. The great resort of company to the Théâtre Français, considered to be the best of all, has rendered the feeling of dramatic propriety so general that the French spectator cannot endure a work in which it is not duly observed, whatever may be its other merits.'

Rameau

In most cases I shall pass pretty rapidly from one composer to another. But the first two or three names on my list demand, from their importance, more than a few hasty words.

I have already explained why Rameau stands alone this evening, and have reminded you that Lulli the Italian was his predecessor and Grétry the Belgian his successor, all three working for the French opera at Paris.

I must now give a short history of this remarkable man Rameau, who both as a theorist and a practical musician fills up a large space in the history of the art. As a theorist he has been regarded as the Newton of music. As a practical musician, he had the power to set aside one of the greatest favorites of the French public (the Italian Lulli) whose firm position it was thought, up to that time, impossible to disturb.

Another remarkable circumstance connected with Rameau is the fact that with all the powers he is known to have felt himself possessed [of], he did not compose his first opera (Hippolite et Aricie) until he was fifty years of age. Nevertheless, this first attempt immediately commenced the war between his partisans and the partisans of Lulli, and proved a decisive blow.

He continued to work onwards, and the very strong opposition he met with conduced, in the sequel, to his advantage, his former enemies becoming his stoutest admirers. Some of the opinions of the day upon Rameau's music are so strong, and yet given with such humour, that they are frequently quoted. He is said to have overpowered all his predecessors 'by dint of harmony and quantity of notes.'

Rameau accompanied his recitatives with the orchestra, so far making a step in advance of Lulli, who could only sustain his melody with a simple bass, with probably a clavier or harpsichord accompaniment, a plan indeed to be found used in later times and not to be despised, even by Rameau.

The [orchestral] accompaniments of Rameau, however, are spoken of as noisy and in bad taste. At any rate the specimen I have found for this evening does not exhibit him in that light; but what was thought a tempest in those days would probably be considered a calm in ours.

What I most dislike to learn of the character of Rameau is the cold, philosophical way in which he set to work in his art. Rameau had gained such a mechanical faculty in <his own> composition that he has been known to express his willingness to set a newspaper to music, and he appears to have done everything according to rule. His personal character exhibits all this coldness in a still more remarkable degree than his works.

Among other doubtful qualities attributed to him was that of extreme avarice. He cared nothing for reputation, honour, or distinction: all he wanted was money, and he fulfilled his wish by dying a rich man.

I am not fond of introducing much personal history into my lectures, because it is difficult at this distance of time to be sure that the right description has been handed down to us, whereas in the professional reputation of a composer, we have only to study his works as the surest evidence. All things considered, Rameau must have been a remarkable man. Seldom has one musician united in himself such strong and varied powers, and the art is (although indirectly) greatly indebted to his appearance.

The trio from the opera of Dardanus in the list of specimens exhibits, to my mind, great feeling, and if the short intermediate choruses could be realised, would produce a very happy effect.

Trio, 'Par un sommeil' (Dardanus)	Rameau

Méhul

Méhul, who by many is supposed to be a Belgian, was born at Givet in France [in] 1763. He is a composer whom all lovers of music must admire. He is great in most departments of the art. His instrumental works, although not so numerous, are as masterly as those for the theatre. His name as it stands in the programme between Rameau and Boieldieu describes his position exactly, as being between the old and new French schools.

Méhul, from his early association with Gluck, as well as from natural disposition, displayed much more of the deep German feeling than the peculiar brilliant manner of his own country. There must for instance have been a strong difference between him and Grétry. The Parisian critics often complained of Méhul as being too dry and German, and Grétry, who was present at the performance of one of his operas, whispered to the person next him, 'I would give a louis to hear a cricket chirp just now.' Notwithstanding this piece of satire, who would not prefer the reputation of Méhul to that of Grétry?

The opera of Joseph is not unknown in this country, although from its spiritual subject it is rather regarded as an oratorio than an opera. The specimen of Méhul is from Joseph.[1]

Air, 'Champs paternelle' (Joseph)	Méhul

[1] *Joseph* was performed in German at Drury Lane in 1841, and in English at Windsor Castle in 1856 (Loewenberg, *Annals*, cols. 600–1).

Boieldieu, Auber, & Hérold

The names of Boieldieu, Auber, and Hérold come next in order. These three splendid men, as before said, have made the reputation of the modern French school of lyric drama. To them is France, without a shadow of a doubt, indebted for her present eminence in operatic composition.

To me, the epoch of Boieldieu always appears as remarkable as anything to be found in the history of music. Notwithstanding all the influences of Gluck and Méhul in France, and in later times of Cherubini & Rossini, there has arisen a school as new as it is beautiful, and which expresses French feeling and temperament to the very letter.

It will, for the sake of separating the specimens, be necessary to speak a few words individually of these composers. Otherwise, as a matter of history, they need not be disunited.

Boieldieu, as having the earliest date of birth, comes first in the programme. He began to be known as a dramatic composer about the year 1800, his opera of 'The Caliph of Baghdad' having established his reputation. Two of his operas, 'John of Paris' and 'La dame blanche', are known to the English stage. The last named opera was produced after a long period of silence on the part of its author, and is considered to have greater solidity of style than is to be found in his previous works. Boieldieu died in 1834.

The specimen presented to you this evening is from this opera.

Duet, 'De l'amour' (La dame blanche)	Boieldieu

Auber, now eighty years of age and still living in France, is not inferior to any one of his predecessors or successors. His opera 'La Neige' was produced in 1823 and first brought him into notice. It became 'very popular, not only in France but in England'.

His earlier works are criticised as being too much in the Rossinian style – this, to me, is unaccountable. Auber is a much older man than Rossini, and judging from those works which we so well know, no trace can be found of the Italian manner.

Air, 'Dans ces forêts' (Zanetta)	Auber

Hérold died a young man, a great loss to his country. What he produced during his lifetime gave large promise of a brilliant future. His opera of Marie was produced in 1826 and his opera of Zampa in 1831. Zampa appeared in an English dress at one of our theatres, but it was poorly got up and performed, and consequently had little success.

The specimens from his works, two of which I have selected, are from 'Zampa' and 'La pré aux clercs'; they will be given in succession.

Duo, 'Les rendezvous' (La pré aux clercs)	Hérold
Air, 'Sainte Alice' (Zampa)	Hérold

Halévy, Adam, Félicien David, Berlioz

We come now to composers of somewhat later dates, and possessing somewhat inferior powers, although genius and character are present in a remarkable degree. I regret that time will not allow me to go far into the artistic careers of these composers of opera, but their claims to enquiry are not to be denied.

In the case of Halévy, he takes, perhaps, the most important place after the great men of whom I have been speaking. His operas have made [a] considerable sensation and are acknowledged masterpieces. Halévy's opera of 'La Juive' has been performed in London with <a degree of> success, which was only qualified by the story being entirely unsuitable to the English public.[1] This composer died at Nice, so recently as 1862. The specimen from his works is taken from the opera of 'Guido et Ginevra.'

Air, 'Pendant la nuit' (Guido et Ginevra)	Halévy

Adolphe Adam, Félicien David and Berlioz are composers and musicians of whom France may well boast. Adolphe Adam, the composer of the opera 'La Postillon de Lonjumeau', will for a long time remain a favorite with the musical public. The specimen from his works will do him great justice, as being full of that character which distinguishes him.

Air, 'Qui des choristes' (Le postillon de Lonjumeau)	A. Adam

Félicien David and Hector Berlioz deserve more for their exertions in lyric art than I fear they will ever obtain. I have great esteem for their talent and for their devotion, but I see the impossibility of working out a genius where genius does not exist.

They have both essayed new forms of composition and style. But the epoch of Boieldieu is not yet worn out, and forms, positively new, are not yet wanted. When they are wanted, they are sure to come. So it has always been.

1 See p. 23.

You will hear one specimen from each of these composers, and which specimens will complete my programme for this evening.

Air, 'Sur l'arbre' (Christophe Colombe)	F. David
Air, 'Vallon sonore' (Les Troyens)	Berlioz

Conclusion

You will observe in looking back upon the specimens which have been produced this evening that the composers of these, with the exception of Rameau and Méhul, belong to our own time – indeed, that the eldest of them (Auber) is still alive to adorn the art, and to enjoy that reputation so richly his due. It is true that after Méhul and before Boieldieu, Auber, & Hérold I could have placed a few specimens from such worthy men as Berton, Catel & Le Sueur, but with all respect for what they did in assisting the lyric drama of France, their efforts have left but a faint impression – an impression gradually disappearing.

There is one name however, which, in connection with the modern French composers of opera, cannot be passed over. At this moment, there is a French composer who has taken possession of the lyric stage throughout Europe. I have not given you a specimen of his works, because there must be very few among my audience who are not acquainted with his masterpiece, that work (Faust) which has suddenly (after a series of artistic struggles on his part) presented him with a splendid reputation.

Not from the want of vocal and instrumental illustrators have I abstained from introducing any compositions of Gounod, for I could have found them at the corner of every street on my way here this evening, although they would not have been of the first class.

Seriously speaking, there can be no doubt that the appearance of Gounod will (in his country at least) greatly influence the young composers of his time.

His work (Faust) which has taken such hold on the public contains many beauties, and its general construction is novel and highly effective. The melody is in most cases pure and natural, and the masterly instrumentation of the whole opera performs an immense share in its success. There are fewer grand points than are to be found in the operas of <Méhul,> Boieldieu, Hérold and Auber; Gounod seems satisfied with the power he possesses to keep his audience interested by a perpetual succession of elegant phrases. In fact, I may describe his work as one large piece of incidental music. It remains to be seen what the successors of Gounod will do upon his model. If they can give half the pleasure he has done, they will be heartily welcomed, but it is to be hoped that they will not forget Boieldieu & Auber.

I now take my leave of French composers of opera, paying them my sincere tribute of admiration for all the grand and beautiful things they have done. If they have not the smooth, lovely melody of the Italians, nor the deep feeling of the Germans, they have many qualities in their music, which either nation might envy them.

8

On the Music for the Theatre Composed by Natives of Germany

London Institution, 21 March 1864

I have now arrived at my fourth and last division of composers for the theatre, and the list of this evening will give you names of eminent men, some indeed super-eminent, all born in Germany.[1] As I intend, towards the close of my lecture, to take a short review of the ground we have travelled over since I began the subject, I shall not make any long introduction before proceeding to speak of the composers and their works included in the programme.

I have not thought it necessary to set down for performance specimens from thoroughly well known authors, unless with some very special object. I thought it right, however, that the whole line of German composers for the theatre should be shown, from the time of Handel to the present day.

There can be very little doubt as to the wonderful aid given by composers of Germany to the lyric drama. It is a curious fact that after the invention of the opera at Florence it was a German who made the first attempt to rival the Italian composers. This German composer, whose name was Schütz, composed an opera at Dresden about the year 1628, the libretto of which was identical with that of the first Italian opera ever given, and having the same title – Dafne.[2]

With this exception we do not find that the Germans interfered much with the opera until shortly before the time of Handel, from which time

1 Before the formation of the German Empire in 1870, 'Germany' tended to cover all the German-speaking states, and thus Bennett included composers such as Haydn and Mozart who would now be treated as Austrian.

2 In fact Schütz's *Dafne* was a play in German with musical interludes, to a libretto by Martin Opitz.

indeed may be dated the commencement of their <reign>{labours} as composers for the theatre.

Handel's immediate predecessor was Keiser, born in the year 1673 and who, in his time, had a splendid reputation, now very much faded, [if] not altogether gone. It is said that this Keiser composed one hundred operas and kept possession of the Hamburg stage for more than forty years. If we are to believe the famous Hasse, 'Keiser was one of the greatest musicians the world had ever seen'. This, coming from one who himself was living in the time of Handel, must strike us with astonishment, seeing that the demand for Keiser's music in our day is extremely small, and that any thing which is really good is seldom allowed to escape.

The principal German composers for the theatre contemporary with Handel were Hasse (called by Burney 'Il Signor Hasse') and Mattheson, Handel's friend at Hamburg. Hasse seems to have been too much of a German for the Italians, for they call him 'Il sassone' (the Saxon), and too little of a German for Burney, who {calls him a signore &} gives a splendid account of his visit to Hasse at Vienna in 1773.

A composer who set all the operas of Metastasio to music except one, and some of them three or four times over, besides writing about fifteen oratorios, numerous masses, and a large batch of instrumental music, all of which greatly pleased in his day, deserves recognition, although Hasse with his idol Keiser will be little sought for any more.

If only on account of Hasse's past grand reputation, it is necessary to produce a small specimen of his works. This specimen should come after Handel, but when I begin to speak of Handel I cannot afford to wait for Hasse, so I present him at once.[1]

Air	Hasse

Mattheson, <Handel's friend>, who is now remembered chiefly in regard to the duel which he fought with Handel, was a composer of operas of respectable talent in Hamburg, a talent probably not in the least degree superior to many of his time. Still in his day he performed a good part in the progress of the art, and his connection with Handel always preserves his name from entire oblivion.

[1] In the printed 'Programme' accompanying the lecture Bennett listed untitled 'specimens' by Reiser [sic] and Mattheson, then the Handel excerpt, then the unspecified 'Air' by Hasse. Evidently he changed his mind, either because he could not find suitable pieces by Keiser and Mattheson or because of time considerations.

Handel

We have been so accustomed, and properly so, to think of Handel as associated with that only which is sacred and sublime in music, that it is difficult to realise the fact that the best part of his life was spent almost exclusively in the service of the theatre, not only as one of its chief composers, but also as manager and theatrical agent, making long journeys to engage singers, having the discomfort of the usual green-room squabbles, and finally like most other managers losing his ten thousand pounds.

Handel came to England in the year 1710, being then five & twenty, <but> having already achieved a considerable reputation in his own country, his first opera, 'Almira', having been first produced at Hamburg in the year 1704, his second opera, called 'Nero', soon afterwards.[1]

But before coming to England, Handel paid a visit to Italy, having carefully husbanded his resources for this purpose. He stayed some time at Florence, where he composed the opera of 'Rodrigo'. Thence he went to Venice, where in 1709 he produced his opera of 'Agrippina'. There he met perchance Domenico Scarlatti, the famous son of the famous Alessandro Scarlatti. What would we not have given to have been present at the meeting of these two great clavier (or harpsichord) performers.

Handel then visited Rome, and produced a serenata entitled 'Il Trionfo del Tempo'; after this he proceeded to Naples, where he set music to an Italian libretto of 'Acis and Galatea,' very different from the English drama written by Gay, to which Handel wrote music for the Duke of Chandos at Cannons in the year 1721, and which is the 'Acis and Galatea' so well known and so well-loved by the English musical public. The Italian opera 'Acis and Galatea', under the title of 'Acigi, Galatea, e Polifemo',[2] is to be found in the magnificent collection of Handel's manuscripts in the possession of Her Majesty at Buckingham Palace, where I have had the privilege of examining it. I found little affinity between the English work and the Italian, save one little point connected with a song we all well know, 'Hush, ye pretty warbling choir'. In the Italian opera there are no choruses, but we know there are many in our English 'Acis and Galatea'.

Is it not a grand remembrance that Handel wrote for us an English opera? But we must go back!

When Handel returned to Germany, on quitting Italy in 1710, he went

[1] There are a number of incidental inaccuracies in Bennett's accounts of the careers of the composers in this lecture. They will not, for the most part, be corrected here.

[2] This is the cantata 'Sorge il dì', also titled *Aci, Galatea e Polifemo*.

to Hanover, where he found a magnificent patron in the Elector, who afterwards ascended the English throne as George the First. This prince received Handel very graciously, and wishing ultimately to secure his services, settled on him a pension of 1500 dollars upon condition that he would return to his court, when he had completed his travels.

Handel then, with his new fortune, went to Düsseldorf – the spot where, in our time, the talent & genius of many of the painters and musicians of Europe have been encouraged and fostered, and where Mendelssohn spent some of his happiest years and first produced his 'St. Paul', <at which performance I had the pleasure to be present>.[1]

Handel was now looking forward with impatience to seeing England. He had heard much of our country from several of the nobility whom he had met in Italy and Hanover, and had received pressing invitations from them. He arrived in the year 1710, and his reception was so flattering to him that he at once decided to make England his home, and with the exception of a short visit to Ireland in 1741 never left it again.

But fate had not only decided that Handel should make England his home, but it had also decreed that the Elector of Hanover should become King of England. Handel, who had never fulfilled his promise of returning to the service of the Elector, was conscious of his ingratitude to a prince who had received him with such marks of appreciation and bounty, and durst not approach the court, until a friendly hand paved the way for his return to the favor of the King. Much to the honor of this monarch, he not only readily forgave Handel, but doubled the pension previously bestowed upon him by Queen Anne, with something in addition.

In refreshing my acquaintance with Handel's operas (about 35 in number) for the purpose of this lecture, I have been astonished and delighted with the strength and power contained in them. It would not surprise me if some of them should once more appear on the stage, in which case, should there be found less passion in them compared to modern productions, there would at any rate be found much <more> genuine and beautiful music, such as could only spring from the matchless author of the 'Messiah' and 'Israel in Egypt.'

The specimens from Handel are taken from his opera of 'Giulio Cesare'. They consist of a duett (extremely beautiful in style and which forcibly reminds us of the 'Giovinette' of Mozart [from *Don Giovanni*]), and the last finale <the shape of which could no longer be used by subsequent composers after the reform of Gluck>.

Duetto, 'Caro! più amabile beltà', and Finale (Giulio Cesare)	Handel

[1] This took place at the Lower Rhine Festival on 22 May 1836.

Gluck

Nevertheless, with all the power and genius possessed by Handel so abundantly shown in aftertimes, it never occurred to him to do any thing towards a reconstruction of the lyric drama. This was left to his contemporary Gluck, who worthily fulfilled his mission. Whenever the word 'opera' is pronounced, the name of Gluck should be associated with it.

This great master was one of that class sent to us very rarely – one like Alessandro Scarlatti of former times and Joseph Haydn of after times, clearing the way through an immense amount of material brought together by industrious musical bees, having no settled hive and no power of arrangement.

Gluck's first work for the theatre was his opera of 'Artaxerxes', produced at Milan in 1741. Even in this first essay he depended entirely on his own genius, avoiding the usual routine of other composers – and this was the first indication that he intended to be independent throughout his career and establish his name as an inventor, which he has thoroughly well done.

It must be a source of pride to the English musical public that Gluck confesses, in a conversation with Dr Burney, that he modelled his latest and greatest works according to the prevalent taste of England when he visited it in 1745. At this visit he brought out his opera 'The Fall of the Giants', which was comparatively a failure. Gluck describes the discomfort of his visit, and says that he worked with fear and trembling, having very few friends, and being obliged to compete with Handel, then in high favour with the public. It is said that Handel pronounced Gluck's opera as detestable. On Gluck's return to Germany, he worked out the experience of his visit to England. Burney relates as follows: 'He told me that he owed entirely to England the study of nature in his compositions [. . .] : he remarked particularly what the audience seemed most to feel; and finding that plainness and simplicity had the greatest effect upon them, he had ever since that time endeavoured to write for the voice, more in the natural tones of the human affections and passions, than to flatter the loves of deeper science or difficult execution – and it may be remarked that most of his airs in 'Orfeo' are as plain as English ballad.'[1]

But though Gluck studied simple nature so much in his cantilena or voice part, yet in his accompaniments he is not only learned, but often elaborate: and in this respect he is even more a poet than a musician.

One remarkable feature in the operas of Gluck is the beautiful incidental music, assigned to the orchestra. Specimens of this class are to be

[1] From Burney's *Present State of Music in Germany* (pp. 263–4). Quoted at greater length (and more accurately) in Lecture 2: see pp. 48–9.

found in all his grandest works. It seemed that he was not only anxious to reform operatic vocal music but also to exhibit his power of widening the form of instrumental music, so stiff and formal, even in the works of Handel.

With the aid of my friend Mr Dorrell,[1] a specimen of incidental music shall be presented from his opera of 'Orfeo'.

Incidental Music (Orfeo [ed Euridice])	Gluck

Gluck was a great link between Handel and the next illustrious German we have to speak of.

Haydn

Haydn never seems to be absent when any department of the musical art is mentioned – this composer of about 118 symphonies, 83 quartetts, and a large amount of other grand works, including 'The Creation', 'The Seasons', 'The Last Seven Words' and many other things, is said to have composed about 50 operas for his patron, Prince Esterhazy.[2] Deeply is it to be deplored that nearly the whole of these works were destroyed by a fire in the Prince's house at Vienna.

Haydn like Handel is closely connected with the English musical public, by means of the great works he wrote specially for this country, including his twelve grand symphonies, his canzonets composed to the English words of Mrs Hunter, and several minor instrumental compositions.

It is interesting to know that there are still living some members of the musical profession who can remember Haydn on his visit to England. My venerable and highly respected friend Sir George Smart has often given me a vivid description of the sensation produced by Haydn in the Hanover Square Room, on the occasion of his engagement with Salomon, for whose concerts he composed his grand symphonies.

One opera at least by Haydn is extant, and this is the beautiful work 'Orfeo', written during his residence in England. I am only too happy to be able through the <beautiful> {splendid} song you will hear to present Haydn as a dramatic composer of the highest class.

Aria, 'Cara speme' (L'anima del filosofo [= Orfeo])	Haydn

1 William Dorrell (1810–96) was a lifelong friend and supporter of Bennett's and a distinguished pianist. In this case they played the Gluck excerpt as a piano duet: a note in the text says 'Duett P.F.'

2 On a facing pages Bennett listed five German and twelve Italian operas taken from Haydn's own catalogue of his works.

Winter

Winter, although not to be tested by the high standard of Mozart and Haydn, is nevertheless entitled to a lofty position among the standard composers of opera. In his own country he is reckoned scarcely inferior to any lyric composer, and in this country his music was formerly well known and greatly admired. His visit to England in the year 1804 caused a great sensation, and the operas which he composed expressly for the King's Theatre met with enormous success. Among these were the operas of Zaira, Proserpina and Calypso, in which Mme Grassini, Mrs Billington and Braham performed. As a specimen of the tender feeling to be found in Winter's music, we will take a short specimen from his opera of 'The interrupted sacrifice'.

Air [(Das unterbrochene Opferfest)]	Winter

Apart from his distinguished position as a composer, Winter was celebrated as one of the greatest violinists of his time, and in this double capacity he reminds us of one who will come before us presently, the great Louis Spohr.

Mozart

It will not be necessary for me to press the claims of Mozart upon your notice or to say many words upon his music.

The most interesting fact that connects Mozart with us is the visit he paid to London in the year 1764. I never go through Frith Street, Soho, without wondering which was the house where Mozart with his father lodged. Mozart was received with great kindness in England, especially by the King (George the 3rd), which his father warmly acknowledges in a letter to the mother at home. There seems some good authority for stating that this visit made such an impression upon Mozart that in later life he entertained the idea of settling in England.

The first opera composed by Mozart as a mere child was ordered by the Emperor Joseph the 2nd, but was never performed or published. One of his earliest operas after this was the Seraglio, a work although written it is said at the early age of fourteen or fifteen, is not in some respects excelled by those operas of Mozart of later date. I will just stop my remarks to bring forward a specimen.

Trio [?'Marsch, marsch, marsch'] (Die Entführung)	Mozart

I feel that I lay myself open to the charge of impertinence if I venture to point to the shadow of a deficiency in the dramatic genius of Mozart, but it has been remarked by more than one, that the tone of his comic operas is far too sombre, and that in this respects he is surpassed by his {more} volatile successor Rossini.

Certainly we find some very serious airs and concerted music in situations which scarcely seem to justify them, and we often find extreme dignity in place of archness, but these are faults, if faults at all, on the right side. The grandest and most dramatic of all the works of Mozart are unquestionably the 'Idomeneo' and the 'Clemenza di Tito'.[1]

Himmel

On my way I must pay a passing tribute to the elegant composer of Fanchon.

Himmel was a musician of no ordinary stamp, and apart from composing for the theatre, he wrote also for the church. He paid a visit to England in the year 1801, but there are no particulars existing as to this visit, at least, I have been unable to find them.[2]

Beethoven

As in the case of Mozart, I need not dwell much upon the name next in the list. Beethoven is known to us more as an instrumental composer than as a composer for the theatre. His only opera 'Fidelio' makes us greatly regret that his contributions have not been more numerous, but there is a large amount of incidental operatic music of the highest interest which should be known by all lovers of the art. On Mendelssohn's visit to the Philharmonic Society some years since the incidental music in the 'Ruins of Athens' was performed for the first time in England, and last year was performed at the Philharmonic Soc[iety] the incidental music in 'Egmont'.

One of the most beautiful specimens of dramatic music in existence, is that which you will hear from 'Fidelio'.

Quartett[3] (Fidelio)	Beethoven

1 For comment see the Introduction, p. 23.

2 *Fanchon das Leyermädchen* was premiered at Berlin in 1804. Bennett's printed programme lists an unnamed 'specimen' by Himmel.

3 There is nothing to indicate whether this was the Act I quartet ('Mir ist so wunderbar') or the one from Act II ('Er sterbe!').

Hummel

One is glad to be able to include in the list of composers for the theatre the name of the accomplished Hummel, who has worthily filled a most distinguished position in the art of music. Hummel, without much strength or originality in his works, is a beautiful example to young composers of elegance and finish. This composer came to England as Master Hummel in the year 1791 and remained two years. As a pianoforte player he was one of the [most] finished and graceful it has ever been my fortune to hear.

The specimen from his opera of 'Matilda von Guise' will perhaps make you anxious to become acquainted with the entire work – although its subject may remind you of something well known to England & Scotland.

Song, 'L'ombrosa notte'[1] (Matilda von Guise)	Hummel

Spohr and Weber

We come now to two names next on the list, names which can never be forgotten while the art exists. Spohr and Weber, as you will see, came into the world at about the same time. Now I would not for a moment compare Spohr with Weber as a genius, but of genius Spohr had a very large share, and as a master of his art, I have no hesitation in placing him first. It has always struck me as a remarkable fact that these men should have had the mission to bring all that richness of harmony into music, so fascinating to young composers, and yet in themselves remain so distinct. Spohr is so individual that even Weber, appearing almost at the same moment, could not eclipse him, and he never will be eclipsed. With regard to Weber I have no hesitation in pronouncing him one of the greatest geniuses we have ever known, if not the greatest.[2]

Spohr's music is so much less known than that of Weber that whilst I find it unnecessary to mention any of the works of the composer of Oberon and Der Freyschütz, I feel it a duty to draw your attention to the large contributions make by Spohr to the lyric drama. The opera best known to the English public is that of 'Azor and Zemira' produced at Covent Garden with great success some years since; but there are many other beautiful operas composed by Spohr, among which we find Macbeth, Jessonda, Pietro von Abano, The Alchymist, and Faust – these

1 An Italian version of the romanze, 'Geheimnissvolle Nacht'.

2 The printed programme lists an unnamed 'specimen' by Weber.

works are well known to the German stage, but always require first-rate performance.

In selecting a short specimen of Spohr for this evening, I confess to an intention of reminding you that there is another Faust in existence besides that of Gounod.

Duet, 'Dearest let thy Footsteps'[1] (Faust)	Spohr

Marschner

As a composer for the theatre Marschner is extremely popular in Germany and indeed elsewhere. His opera of the 'Templar and the Jewess' always attracts a large audience. His opera of the Vampyr was produced in England some years since and met with great success. His style is modelled upon that of Weber, although possessing sufficient originality to maintain for him a worthy place in the art. Marschner visited England about six or seven years ago and died at Hanover soon afterwards.

The song which you will hear in one of the choicest examples of Marschner which I could find, and it is published in the English form in which you will hear it.

Song, 'From the ruin's topmost tower'[2] (Der Vampyr)	Marschner

[Mendelssohn]

Mendelssohn's operettas, made for the occasional festivals at his parents' home, scarcely come under the list of public theatrical music, but they are very beautiful, as everything must be which comes from his pen. The finale to 'Lorelei', the only published fragment from that contemplated opera, shows us distinctly what a gift Mendelssohn would have bestowed upon us had he been spared & finished this, his first great theatrical work. As it is, we ought to be deeply grateful to him for the beautiful incidental music in the Midsummer Night's Dream and for his choruses in the great plays. Mendelssohn could make no failure in whatever he undertook. It is well known that one of his intentions was to compose an opera on the subject of Shakespeare's 'Tempest'.[3]

1 'Folg' dem Freunde', as translated by Edward Taylor.

2 'Dort an jenem Felsenhang', as translated by J. R. Planché.

3 The printed programme lists an unnamed 'specimen' by Mendelssohn, presumably from *Lorelei*.

Wagner

Had this lecture been given some two or three months later we should have been better prepared to discuss the merits of Richard Wagner as a composer for the theatre. Speaking for myself I greatly regret that I have not yet had an opportunity to hear any thing of Wagner's in its proper place, and it is not fair to judge him by the rare pianoforte arrangement of his works. We are promised a complete and grand performance of his opera of 'Tannhäuser' this season, and there is no doubt that the production of this work will excite the deepest interest.[1] In Germany the enthusiasm with which this work is received is indescribable – but whatever may be the verdict of the English public, I for one shall accept it as a just one. There is no doubt that the thorough German character of the story has much to do with the success of Wagner's opera in his own country. The overture to this work has often been played and has become well known.

Although I have put no specimen from Wagner down in the programme, I think an appropriate ending to those remarks and to my specimens would be a performance of the march in the opera of which we have been speaking.

March from Tannhäuser	Wagner

Conclusion

I have not much time {left} to perform my promise of taking a review of the ground we have travelled over during the four lectures. But I should wish to remind you of one or two points <connected with our subject> which have arisen during our enquiry into the invention of the opera and into the works of those who have aided it.

Will you then remember that the opera form was invented at Florence, that the composer of the first opera 'Dafne' was Peri, that at a later time the great benefactor among the Italian composers was Alessandro Scarlatti? Among the Germans no one can deny the superior claim of Gluck. Among the French must be remembered the names of Boieldieu, Herold, and Auber. With regard to the Belgian composers of opera, you will remember that I expressed my idea that should any new school of dramatic music now arise, it will come from Belgium.

I have been several times asked during my course why I omitted the

1 In fact *Tannhäuser* would not be staged in London until 1873. As already stated, the first British stage performance of any Wagner opera was still in the future: *Der fliegende Holländer*, produced at Drury Lane Theatre in 1870, in Italian as 'L'Olandese dannato'.

lyric composers of England in my scheme. Now I am perfectly aware that England can exhibit many composers whose works would bear favorable comparison with those of other countries. We have only to mention the name of Purcell, then Arne, afterwards Bishop, and in later time Balfe, {John Barnett, [Henry] Smart,} Wallace and Macfarren, to put in a strong claim for Englishmen. A programme of very fine specimens might soon be found from these eminent men, but not even the satisfaction of hearing such good music could tempt me to become, in a manner, the critic of English musicians, especially in the case of those still living.

I must however confess that when invited to give the present course of lectures, the subject of opera music suggested itself to me as one of great interest in England at the present time. It is interesting on many grounds. It is a species of entertainment on which more money is spent than on any thing else in the way of music. There are remarkable facts connected with the state of the lyric drama in London at this moment. The managers of the best conducted English opera house ever known in England are now resigning their positions, having, it is feared, been but inadequately rewarded for their exertions to please the public. On the other hand, nothing daunted, a new company has started with the promise to do everything that can possibly be desired. According to the prospectus, having closely watched all the shortcomings and failures of every theatre up to the present time, it is prepared with means to avert all disaster and to secure without fail the remunerative patronage of the public.[1]

Alas! Let us look back even to the time of Handel the manager.

Again we have two grand establishments for the performance of the lyric drama in the Italian language. These theatres, as I have remarked in a former lecture, can only be Italian by name – they cannot be so in manner. The composer and performers who support the musical entertainment come now from all parts of the continent, perhaps from anywhere rather than from Italy. It was this fact which led me to adopt the plan of classifying the composers under the countries in which they were born rather than the school in which they worked.

There is an evident confusion of styles both in composition and performance in the present day, and although this may arise from an over-abundance of good material, and therefore [be] very hopeful for the future, it will require the strong hand of a Scarlatti or a Gluck to reduce this musical chaos into order.

In the case of our own native composers for the theatre it is now

[1] After the collapse of the Pyne-Harrison opera company, which produced English operas at Covent Garden from 1857 to 1864, the formation an English Opera Association was announced in April 1864. As Bennett's sardonic comments seem to predict, it too would fail in March 1866 (Scholes, *Mirror*, 232).

complained (with what justice I will not enquire) that the model of opera they choose is rather the creation of the publishers than of their own imagination.

But it must be remembered that the cultivation of music in this or any other country is in a great measure in the hands of the public, which decides the direction of art whether for good or evil. Composers like others have to gain their bread by their vocation. 'They who live to please, must please to live.'[1] If the public will not encourage the full development of their talents, and [will] be even more content with the shell than the kernel, can it be wondered at that our music shops are teeming with light productions rather than with thoughtful music? Still, all this is improving rapidly – and I conclude by saying that most of the composers I have mentioned during my course should be known and appreciated by all lovers of art, not only for what they [have] done for the gratification of past time, not only for the gratification which we (of the present day) receive from them, but also that their compositions will supply delight and enjoyment to our children's children, destined as many of them are to remain as models of art and science for ages to come.

1 Also quoted in Lecture 3, p. 67.

PART THREE

Lectures at Cambridge University, 1871

9. Bennett in his academic robes, about 1870

The hood appears to be that of Master of Arts, an unusual honour for a professor of music at Cambridge. The degree was conferred on Bennett in 1867.

9

Music of the Present Time

Arts School?, Cambridge, January 1871?[1]

I purpose in my first lecture this term to begin at the very beginning & root of the matter we have in hand; and therefore, before we proceed to speak about the technicalities of music, and the different works of the great masters, it will be better for us to consider what the present state of the musical world really is, and in what way the minds of musical people are trained to receive the education offered to them in the art.

Never in the history of music was there a period of greater interest than the present. The rapidity with which the various phases of the art are developing themselves (whether in a right or wrong direction), the ceaseless activity of composers, performers & publishers, the enormous increase of the musical public, all these things point out to us the fact that the musical art is in a state of transition & that we may assuredly look for an early & radical change.

Now today let us examine more closely some of the various signs by which this change is most surely indicated, and first let us look to the present German school of music.

The German school <always> {in the last century} had an enormous influence on the young composers who strove to model themselves to the forms built for them by Haydn; but now the young composers of the day are struggling to become original & to find out new forms & to free themselves from those upon which even Beethoven & Mendelssohn were content to work.

Perhaps this state of things may be traced to the influence of such a composer as Wagner <over the present state of music>[2], who possesses an influence hardly to be calculated. His power is extreme; the fasci-

[1] For dating see the Introduction, p. 15.

[2] At this point in the rough draft of the lecture was added 'and other composers junior to him'.

nation which he throws over the musicians of his own country & the musicians of other countries goes even beyond that which Weber in this same department {(I mean the music of the theatre)} was ever able to exercise.

Night after night the same opera and the same audience! and the same deep and mysterious approbation! I have often asked this question but without an answer: In what consists the enchantment of the music? It is not music which comes home to you or into your home; it will not bear as far as I can understand it anything like a reduced shape. It vanishes if removed from its lofty and sumptuously decorated temple, which Wagner never fails to have placed at his disposal. But still its mysterious influence remains.[1]

Next, as another sign of the change, let us look at the immense musical gatherings which now so frequently take place. In these gatherings we, for the most part, find a large & unevenly balanced force employed. For an example of this, let us take one of the Handel Festivals at the Crystal Palace and compare it with the state of things when Handel himself lived.

Handel, sitting at his harpsichord, was content to have a small force arranged around him, which he could control by sign or outspoken voice, his orchestra consisting in all (including instrumentalists, solo vocalists, and chorus) of about 50 performers, Handel himself, as we see by his figured bass, supplying the harmony not appropriated to the instrumentalists in the score.[2]

This eminent Anglo-German living quietly in Brook Street, Grosvenor Square, was little aware of the vast performances in store for his works, and that no limit would be marked either in trouble or expense to proclaim him to the world as an immortal master.

How different the scene from that of 'Cannons', near Edgware, the seat of his friend & patron, the Duke of Chandos.[3] Any young student in music might well take an instructive lesson on going into the Chapel in

[1] Bennett could not have experienced such Wagner-worship personally. It suggests the atmosphere of Munich in the later 1860s. J. W. Davison, who was present at the premiere of *Das Rheingold* on 22 September 1869, sent a totally condemnatory review to *The Musical World*, but he added: 'There are, however, some people who really admire Richard Wagner, who believe him a true prophet and follow him as one who leads to a musical Paradise. These are "the faithful", whose faith is now being tried as by fire.' Bennett, who was a close friend of Davison with similar views of the musical scene, offers a milder and kinder version of the same. (Davison's review is reprinted in Reid, *The Music Monster*, 198–201.)

[2] In comparison, the Handel performances at the Crystal Palace festival of 1859 used 2,765 voices and 457 instrumental players as well as a huge organ (see Musgrave, *Musical Life of the Crystal Palace*, 39).

[3] The chapel no longer stands; the organ case is now in the church of Great Witley, Worcs.

which the oratorio of 'Esther' was first performed. He would see at a glance the proportions with which Handel was satisfied. He would see the almost 'box' organ at which Handel presided, and on which (a brass plate gravely will inform him) 'the oratorio of Esther was composed' (I trust to the intelligence of the student not to take in this information – oratorios & symphonies are not composed either on pianofortes or organs).[1]

I must not be understood to mean that no addition to the original number of the performers should be made, but I certainly think it becomes a question whether the utmost limit as regards the number of performers has not been reached, as unity of execution must in these large gatherings be certainly sacrificed to <immense volumes of sound> {unwieldy force}. This brings me again to my incidental complaint of the unevenly balanced force employed. I wish to draw the attention of the musical student to the watchfulness & carefulness which he should give to the additions to any such primitive scores as those of Handel or Bach. These additions appear now to be a necessity. It must be confessed that such additions are very often overdone and done without judgment.

The force may not be too large but the injudicious choice of additional instruments, whether of the soft or loud species, often on the one hand takes away from the crispness of the author's original instrumentation, while on the other hand a vulgar noise is heard from instruments which the composer might himself have used had he been so inclined, seeing that they were in existence in his time.[2]

Again let us look to the change in the instruments themselves: the increased advantages in the mechanism of instruments which allow orchestral players to play that which at one time would not have been attempted. Look at the increased means open to the hands of the pianoforte player, who has now about two octaves and a half at his service beyond that which was allowed to Beethoven in many of his early sonatas.[3]

I think that as there are two sides to every question it is a matter for our deep thought whether the great additions to these instruments have

1 This is a jocular reference to the academic practice, still intact at Cambridge in the later 20th century, that a student of composition must learn to compose in the head without the assistance of an instrument, and to write out the result directly on music paper. It suggests, though hardly proves, that some members of the audience were studying composition privately with Bennett.

2 Bennett probably had in mind trombones, serpents, and side drums, all in use at the Crystal Palace festivals.

3 Most Viennese pianos in the 1790s had a compass of five octaves (FF–f‴) and Beethoven did not exceed these limits in his sonatas for piano solo until Op. 53, published in 1805. In Bennett's time some pianos already had the modern compass of a little over seven octaves.

led so much to a right end as they ought to have done, [or] whether they have not rather led to the introduction of a kind of music which is composed more for the sake of showing off the mechanical skill of the performer than for the sake of furthering the true end of musical composition. When we hear the sublime and solid models composed by men who had no other means at command for their performance than the old clavier, as I said before I think this is a subject which demands our most serious attention. Let us remember the introduction of new instruments into our orchestras, [and] the disappearance of others, such as the real trumpet and the bass & alto trombones.

Another subject which has engrossed the mind of the musical public is the increased height[1] of the pitch of our orchestras compared to that of 25 years since. The serious effect this must have on the performance of compositions of the past & what a new state of things it must introduce as regards the music of the future is evident. And now as another great sign of the change, let us consider the individuality of the different schools, and let us first look at Italy.

Italy has given us as models Palestrina, Carissimi, the two Scarlattis (father & son), Clari, Corelli, and many others scarcely less brilliant. We ought to look with grateful feelings to a land which for centuries upheld the grandeur & true spirit of music. Still it must be a matter of disappointment that the Italian composers of the present day are more actively employed in subserving the demands of fashion than in following the true end of art.

Step by step[2] has weakness overtaken the composers of music for the theatre in Italy. Bit by bit are they yielding their proud position until at last their almost final extinction is by many proclaimed, but should the oft repeated saying in their case be verified ('Wherever an art has fallen, the blame rests with the artists'), there are many friends of Italian music who would deplore this state of things.

The Italian composers have still that intuitive feeling for melody of which, it seems, no fate can deprive them; they have enriched their works with greater variety of colouring & harmony than can be found in the works of their predecessors, but they are fast losing form & outline and the elaboration indispensable in works destined to become famous.

Here is a case of degeneracy it would be wrong to disguise. In fact the individuality of the Italian school has almost entirely disappeared. Still I

1 The original phrase (deleted in the rough draft) was 'frightful height'. For often obscure reasons, pitch standards have varied from time to time and from place to place; it appears that in Victorian England there was a noticeable rise in pitch, to as high as $a' = 452$ hertz.

2 This paragraph, the next, and part of the next are identical to the concluding passage of Lecture 6, p. 103.

cannot leave this school, in gratitude for what it has already done, without a hope that its extinction may be yet remote, although the most successful writers for the Italian stage are {now} either French or German composers, while the performers are collected from all parts of the world.

The French school seems to have preserved its individuality above other countries, and was for a long time impervious to outside influence, but even in France a giving way is now noticeable. Up to a very few years ago this wonderfully artistic & musical people had given only one performance of the Messiah. Now concerts have been recently established in Paris for European music & European composers. These performances have led to the introduction of many compositions produced with great success & previously unknown to the French people. In fact nationality or individuality in music is fast disappearing, & perhaps altogether this is not to be regretted. Let it not be understood that I am referring to national songs, which I sincerely hope nations may keep. This may be considered a sarcastic wish since those people[s] who possess national songs in most abundance are the least educated in art.

In secular vocal music there is a wonderful mixture of sentimentality & vulgarity, and it is sad to think of the immense amount of money paid by the public upon this department of music.[1] It is without force & character & (in England especially) is too much encouraged over that which is healthy & characteristic.

England & English musicians may well deplore the <decadence> {decay} of one branch of music in which she achieved eminence and has left her mark. I mean the school of glee writing. Students in music will be doing well not to pass over too lightly this school, which is now for a time clouded over by the shower of part songs so abundantly teeming from music shops. The form of the latter is trivial compared to the solid earnestness and musicianship of glee writers such as Webbe, Callcott, Horsley, Attwood & others down to Bishop, at which point the school seems to have terminated.

The text of these glees was for the most part chosen with great good taste & discretion & no haste discovered in the music. Although the term 'glee' was in many cases a misnomer, it was universally accepted and applied to many thoughtful & serious works of art (for such they really can be called) as well as to those of a cheerful & joyous character. The part songs of the present day have considerably less value when measured by an artistic standard.

1 The following sentence, inserted here in the rough draft, was later deleted: 'You may be passing on your way to a performance of the Philharmonic Society at St. James' Hall and find the Christy Minstrels refusing admission from the overcrowded rooms.' For Christy Minstrels see Scott, 'Blackface Minstrels'.

Is there not a change (at any rate in England) going on in cathedral & church music? – the modern and more melodious (though not always the more masterly) compositions superseding those which may be described as of the dry scholastic manner of the older writers of church music?

It must however be remembered that even in what I have called the dry days of church music, there are composers – Purcell, Weldon, etc. – whose works are intensely pathetic & in a certain sense melodious, and whose compositions, it is hoped, will be exempted from the general destruction of a school which is already showing decay.

And now to come to church psalmody. The change in this has been immense. It has advanced with such rapid strides that it is almost a question whether the state of confusion into which it has fallen is any improvement on the old state of things, bad as they were.

The crude & chromatic harmonies which one now finds in church psalmody are but unsuccessful imitations of John Sebastian Bach, who when he employed his harmonies wrote them for skilled vocalists and not for a general congregation. The harmonised chorales of this great master are to be found in a collection of 371 called the 'Choral Gesänge'[1] and which are studded about in his numerous works and, I may add, are now being (often in a mutilated shape) introduced into parish churches.[2] These chorales have incited young musicians to all sorts of crudities – chromatic harmonies and ornamental notes, being used without any sort of feeling or scholarship.

As further distinct evidence of the conflict and agitation now going on, it can be pointed out that while on the one hand the effusions of the ultra German school, which deeply affect young students here and elsewhere, appear so rapidly: on the other hand, societies are formed for the production in a splendid form of the works of the old & great masters, many of which have not before been published, many of which indeed their composers could scarcely have realised in performance. In Leipzig there is a Bach Society which presents its subscribers annually with a splendid volume of Bach's <u>almost</u> unknown works & in some cases <u>quite</u> unknown. These are published with a regularity and accuracy that would make one imagine the composer himself to be the editor. Bach's fate as an artist was so widely different to that of Handel that I cannot help alluding to it under the argument of a new state of things in music. The old cantor

1 *Joh. Seb. Bachs vierstimmige Choral-gesänge*, ed. J. P. Kirnberger and C. P. E. Bach, 4 vols. (Leipzig, 1784–87).

2 Despite Bennett's own meticulous editorial work in *The Chorale Book for England* (London: Longman, Green, 1863), which probably antedated this lecture, a number of greatly altered versions of Bach's chorale harmonisations were in use. *Hymns Ancient & Modern* (London: William Clowes & Sons, 1861) carried four specimens, all of them 'adapted'; they were reprinted in 1868.

of the Thomas School at Leipzig, with his inherent faith and modesty in his art, when once fixed in that city, with his good organ, with his large school quire (an institution which exists to this day), with some at least of his 20 musical children round about him, {busy} copying, engraving, instructing at the same time, cared not for the public. He produced weekly {for the Thomas Church} splendid specimens of his genius and solid musicianship, which his quire (though a small force) could perform decently. He could however only realise his vast conceptions in this small way, & to the general public they were as a sealed book.

How different to the case of Handel. He was constantly writing for the public & watching the effect he was making. For these reasons (and they must be stated with great hesitation), the form of Sebastian Bach in many of his large choral works cannot be perpetuated,[1] while those of Handel, by no means superior in theme, poetry, tenderness, and mastery, will not be superseded for ages to come, save in some small details which are beginning to adjust themselves.

And now that we have considered (though but briefly & imperfectly) the signs of the change, it may be as well to try and think how this change may be directed for evil or for good. Whenever in the 'history of music' materials were becoming too abundant, and wanted moulding, master hands were found who set things in order and framed models by which younger students might form their works & become true disciples of the art. Such men were Alessandro Scarlatti, Gluck, and Haydn. They have had glorious followers, who wished to be under no other banners. The next general may be long awaited, but he must surely come. May the next pioneer of music have such grand disciples as Mozart, Spohr and Mendelssohn, and then he will not have come in vain.

The splendid career of Felix Mendelssohn repelled invaders into the art with which they were, for the most part, imperfectly acquainted. They could not touch him, but when he was taken from us, a host of <second-rate> {eccentric} musicians asserted their claims.

Who knows but that Mendelssohn with all his great power might have inaugurated a new form of opera – somewhat foreshadowed by the finished extract of Lorelei. His march was always onward {and always in a true direction}. He was thoroughly conversant with all the music of the past and must have had the keenest eye to the future. Since his death, a terrible havoc has taken place in the art, and to his death I trace the confusion of the art as it at present stands.

1 This prediction was, of course, to prove unfounded. It was probably motivated by the difficulties that had beset Bennett's pioneering performances of the *St. Matthew Passion* in 1854 and their failure to encourage performances by other groups (Bennett, *Life*, 233–5). The rapid rise in interest in Bach's choral works in England began in 1870 under the leadership of Joseph Barnby (Scholes, *Mirror*, 72–4).

But too much confusion is generally the forerunner of order. And this brings me to a few words I wish to say in conclusion, and if a long experience and an active life in music for a great many years give me any claim to offer advice to young musicians, let me do so now.

How much do I wish that young musicians would make themselves more thoroughly acquainted with the glorious and lucid works of Haydn, Mozart, Beethoven, Spohr & Mendelssohn, before entering into that 'Will o' the Wisp' school now so prevalent and so fascinating. Older musicians are much safer from the influence of this sorcery, through their being fortified by their intimacy with the works of those composers to whom I draw attention – they, through their extended experience are able to cull that which is good from that which is worthless. Many young men in all countries are seeking for a reputation at the least trouble and the least cost – they rush at once into the high road of music (as they believe it) and expect to 'awake and find themselves famous', their starting point being nothing short of the 9th symphony of Beethoven, from which point they are ready to follow any magician who offers them an easy success.

Do they believe that without any real toil they can emulate Mr Wagner's position in the art? Do they ever think that to write a decent quartett in proper form would bring them a reward which they might accept with good conscience? What is the use of dealing with unlimited ophicleides, trombones, valve horns, trumpets, harps, drums, &c, if the composer who employs them cannot produce a single theme in his work which the hearer can understand or take away <with him>?

I have met with cases of young students who have shown me their pompous scores, but who were unable to tell me how many symphonies Beethoven {or Mozart} wrote or could give any acceptable description of them. They were content to be musicians of the future.[1]

Let then students in music be more patient in their work, taking to those beautiful specimens of the art which are to hand as models, not attempting to do that in twelve months which would take many years to accomplish, and let them, if in their life they have the responsibility of imparting the principles of their art to others, strive to place before their pupils those works of the great masters which have endured unchanged through many ages, and not lead them astray towards those which are not lasting and which the fickleness of fashion may sweep away with a breath for ever. The orchestral and pianoforte works of Haydn and Mozart, their quartetts, the operas of Gluck, the clavier music of Handel, Scarlatti the younger, and Sebastian Bach, with much fine music given to the world by the children of this great composer, should not be ignored

[1] This refers, of course, to the *Zukunftmusik* movement led by Wagner and Liszt.

by those students who wish to cultivate a <true and> refined taste. It is time <, as I have said before,> that the form in which some of the old masters wrote, is no longer to be employed, but the beauty of the themes and the exquisite harmonies which they used together with the smooth and graceful part writing always to be found in their works render them fine models for a young musician to study.

Still a few words to the student in music, which are sincerely felt. My conviction is that young musicians hasten too soon from their studies to place themselves before the public, whence there is no returning.

True it is that the public is no bad master, but a pupil coming forward must be well prepared – at least with technical skill. In many cases a hasty appearance results in a failure which influences the career of a young musician for life.

Nothing can be done without long and patient <study> {labor}. Close {& dry} study of the art will stand students in good stand, when weak imitations of an eccentric school will bring them into ridicule.[1]

I propose to devote my second lecture to the best advice I can give upon the art of composition, illustrating as far as the means at my disposal allow some of the works of the great masters.[2]

1 This is followed by the beginning of a sentence, later deleted: 'Perhaps the believers in this school, the modern Germans and their English co-believers'.

2 This paragraph appears, together with a deleted earlier version of the same, on a page to itself. It is hard to be sure whether it is the concluding paragraph of Lecture 9 (as it is shown here) or the beginning of a second lecture that was later abandoned. Some notes on harmony and counterpoint are found earlier in the volume, but no complete lecture on the art of composition.

10

Fashions in Music

Arts School?, Cambridge, January 1871?[1]

Introduction

It appears that no art can be exempt from the powerful influence of fashion – I use the word in its old sense.[2] Barely has any artist been able to resist the accepted fancies of his day.

In all arts 'conventionality' will be found. You will notice how the poets of a certain time could not commence a work without an invocation to the muse, or a grand compliment to a patron. To find a similar mannerism in another art – sculpture – pay a visit to Westminster Abbey and look at the works of sculptors who lived in the same period. My duty however is with music, and I wish to say a few words & mention a few examples to show how musicians, and some of the greatest, have been influenced by the fancies of the day.

Let me at once give you an example of what I am trying to do. What could have suggested to Handel to introduce a minuet into the oratorio of Samson? and yet there you find it! It is true that Samson is not strictly a sacred oratorio, not being entirely written to sacred words,[3] but the reason of Handel having introduced the minuet is not to be traced to this. It is to be accounted for by the fashion of the day which could scarcely get on without this sort of movement.

[1] For dating see the Introduction, p. 15.

[2] The 'old sense' of *fashion*, in use from the mid-16th century, was 'the mode of dress, etiquette, furniture, speech, etc. prevalent at a particular time.' A newer sense which dated from the early 19th century was probably the one that Bennett wished to avoid implying here: 'Fashionable people; the fashionable world', with its additional implications of social snobbery. ('Fashion', senses 6b and 6d, *The New Shorter Oxford English Dictionary*, Oxford, 1993.)

[3] A 'sacred oratorio', to the Victorians, meant one that was based strictly on biblical texts. The only Handel oratorios that meet this definition are *Messiah* and *Israel in Egypt*; the rest, including of course *Samson*, are settings of custom-made librettos in verse.

In making a short enquiry into the subject of musical form, I shall not go back farther than to the time of Bach & Handel, for at this period music began to assume a definite shape.

What was the design of the time?

Instrumental music had made so far a stride as to present a boldly constructed first movement. This movement, according to the fashion of the day and for many a day afterwards, consisted of an introductory slow or 'grave' movement followed by a fugue. These movements were supplemented by a series of [pieces of] dance music, and such was the fashion that no composition would be agreeable to the ears of the public of that day unless built upon the form I have described.

One very interesting point occurs to me in looking back at composition of this period: I mean the fashion of dotted notes being used in the introductory movements almost without exception. You will see what I mean by looking at the overtures to Esther, Samson, the Messiah & in fact in nearly all the works of Handel and Bach & their predecessors.

Handel has escaped from this habit in the overture to 'Acis & Galatea', and how startling & beautiful is the idea!

All the composers who lived in the time of Handel & Bach wrote upon the model I have described. Many of these composers are now long forgotten. The 'fashion' of the day did not help them in the long run. Bach in development & continuity seemed greatly superior to Handel & was evidently trying to escape from the fetters of fashion, but this is not the time to talk of this: it would lead into another enquiry.

A few words may be devoted to the fashion of 'opera' composition of that period. Of course the operas of Handel judged at this time are gems compared to those of his rivals. But still they are small in construction, and only kept in remembrance by the many beautiful and vigorous solo songs to be found in them. The works of his rivals, all written according to the fashion of the day, and which caused so much contention at the time, have all disappeared.

It is surprising that Handel could not break through the fashion as Gluck very soon did – and which Handel was alive to witness. Young composers should study closely the works of this great master (Gluck), who was one of the greatest benefactors to the art the world has known. Gluck entirely ignored fashion & produced a design which passed down to Mozart, and from Mozart to a host of minor composers, many of them excellent in their way, such as Cimarosa & Paisiello. On went the form which Gluck inaugurated, up to the advent of Rossini, a composer who feared & cared for nothing, and therefore who has been accepted as a genius rather than as a model. Yet what a powerful man he was and what a host of imitations immediately sprang up, making their bravuras on his plan, using the final cadence which may be called his (and which is now becoming intolerable), in fact trying to get a reputation by a very short process.

That Rossini made a school and was a mannerist cannot be denied. Still how clearly did he show his power of escaping into something of the highest form by producing the 'Guillaume Tell'.

In looking back to the works of Rossini, one is astonished to find the almost light and merry overture to his most tragic operas such as 'Semiramide' and 'Otello'. These are very characteristic specimens of the man.

Repeats: One of the most extraordinary marks of fashion in the history of music is the custom of making (so-called) 'repeats.' This is to allow a great part of a movement to be performed and then once more to return to the beginning. This practice was prevalent in the days of Handel & Bach and in certain compositions of modern authors is brought down to the present day – these repeats will be found in such works as the sonatas of Haydn, Mozart, Beethoven and in the symphonies of the same masters and in those of Mendelssohn.

What would be thought of a poet who having recited the first hundred lines of his work suddenly turned back to the commencement? And yet this practice is constant in music, and at present giving only a few signs of its becoming wearisome.

Not only are the <u>first</u> parts of a movement repeated now according to the expressed signature of the composer, but even his wish is shown for a repetition of the second portion – in fact going through the whole work twice. I am not sure that the latter plan would not be better than that of repeating the first part only, and thus by giving an undue prominence to one part throwing the whole work out of shape.

The few words I have already spoken apply only to the principal movements of a composition, and it would, I believe, be a thoughtful exercise for a student to consider how far these repeats affect the construction of a composition as a whole. It must be a serious difference to the symmetry of the work, if at the will of a conductor the first part is repeated or not. The first part being repeated with its two necessary themes (called 1st & 2nd subjects) throws a great weight upon the second part, which usually contains the elaboration of the subjects. After the elaboration, return is made to the principal subject (generally at least in modern masters), and thus with the first part repeated all the principal subjects are heard three times.

The matter is very different looking at a composition upon paper, where the proportions seem quite consistent; about one third being devoted to the first part of a movement and two thirds to the second part, containing as I have said before, the elaboration of the themes and a return to them in their simple form. When the repeat is allowed, the altered proportions will be easily seen.

It would be unwise to condemn the whole system without due thought & enquiry; these repeats have many powerful friends, and no greater friends than Mendelssohn & Beethoven. But it is a great question whether they were not under the dominion of the custom of the day. Their directions however leave no doubt as to their wishing to have certain large portions of their works repeated: this is shown by bars of music introduced (1st time) for the express purpose of making a smooth return. In these cases it would seem impossible for any conductors to ignore the custom of 'repeats', for by so doing some bars of valuable music would be utterly lost: look to the symphonies of Beethoven & Mendelssohn.[1] In Mozart you find nothing but the ordinary 'repeat' mark, little more in Haydn.

In the great[2] instrumental works, whether for the orchestra or p[iano] forte, there is usually included a movement called either Minuetto, Scherzo, or 'Intermezzo', which in its character is so opposed to all other movements of the composition that its welcome is assured. Its proportions are generally small & strictly rhythmical. Of the repeats of such a movement no one can complain, indeed murmurs would arise if an attempt were made to do away with them.

In my own mind I have little doubt that the matter is purely conventional, and that even these great masters of our time have not escaped the influence of what I choose to call 'fashion in music' – and I use the term in no flippant sense.

I come now to another class of 'repeats': to the 'repeats' in the songs of Handel, Bach, and other masters of the period.

These 'repeats' cannot be reconciled upon any artistic principle. The plan of the composition was this. The greatest and most interesting portion of the song was in the first part, and to all expectation brought to a satisfactory conclusion. But this was not enough for the fashion of the day. An 'episode' came forward, of very slight form and generally, it must be admitted, consisting of tender music, opposed to the principal song – but very short, and only, as it appears, to give a reason for a repetition of the whole of the song. This form has almost cured itself. For few singers can bear the fatigue of singing long & sustained songs twice over, nor can audiences listen with anything like patience.

Then with regard to concertos for solo instruments with full orchestral accompaniments, whether written for the display of a pianist, or violinist, or any other executant: Here you find according to established

1 Another example of this practice is the first movement of Bennett's own Symphony No. 3 in A major, completed in December 1833, which has a 'first ending' of seven bars leading to the repeat of the exposition section. He used plain repeats in the first movements of both symphonies in G minor (those of 1835 and 1864).

2 'great' in the sense of 'large-scale'.

custom (brought down nearly to the present day) a long piece of music acting as a prelude or index to the whole composition. In this prelude, the themes which are afterwards to be employed are, in many compositions, set forth with the dignity and form of a symphony, the orchestra being used with a freedom & grandeur which is denied to it when once the solo performer commences his task.

It is true that in the concertos of Bach & Handel, whether for the organ, clavier, oboe, violin or other instrument, we find an introductory phrase of a few bars given by the orchestra before the solo performer commences, but this introduction is a small affair compared to the so called 'tutti' in modern concertos.

I think there is no doubt that Mozart, in his splendid contribution of upward of twenty pianoforte concertos and concertos for other instruments, inaugurated this design of the long preparatory movements, which many a musician has enjoyed, without perhaps calculating the vast weight which this movement has on all which succeeds it.

Some of these 'preludes' of Mozart, so-called 'tuttis', are some of the finest imaginations of a man who could indeed 'imagine.' At once let me refer you to the 'tuttis' of the first movements of his p[iano]f[orte] concertos in D minor & C minor [K. 466, 491].

Let it be understood that the p[iano]f[orte] in the days of Mozart was not the pianoforte of the present day. At the most, five octaves of keys were at his disposal; we have now seven octaves. For this reason he might have been constantly thinking of the resources always remaining with him of his orchestra, and throwing the 'soloist' not into the 'shade' but into the relief of the composition.

A compensation is found for the comparative background [situation] of the soloist in the opportunity which is invariably left by Mozart at the end of his principal movements for the performer not only to exhibit himself as a thorough master of his instrument, but also as a thorough musician: one who can evince his appreciation of the work which he is interpreting by recalling its themes to the audience, placing them in a fresh light by new keys, new embroidery, and by many subtle contrivances, in fact giving his heart & soul to the work in which he is considered the principal actor.[1]

So strong is 'tradition' that this form of composition has been accepted & adopted by Beethoven, Hummel, Moscheles, Field & many others greatly inferior to them.

Without, at first, speaking of the splendid p[iano] f[orte] concertos of Beethoven one must be reminded of the unique violin concerto of the first named master, with its comprehensive & picturesque prelude, a

[1] This description refers, of course, to the cadenza.

triumph of art, and the violin player must wait and enjoy (as I believe he must always do) several minutes of orchestral work before he puts his bow to the strings, to show that he is after all the principal performer. Again in the pianoforte concertos Beethoven revels in the opportunity given him in the traditional 'prelude' to keep the solo performer in the background until he can appear to the best advantage. True it is, that in two of his finest works of this class, he has successfully broken through the absolute formula of the 'tutti' by introducing the performer even before the prelude, one case to be found in the Concerto [No. 5] in E flat and the other in the Concerto [No. 4] in G major. But still the long 'tutti' is close at hand & is not to be surrendered.

The reflection of a musician will be 'How long can this form of composition last?' Are there any indications of a break off, in this large plan?

As I have said before, not many even of the greatest men are exempt from the 'fashion' of the day, and but a few years since, a young composer essaying to write a concerto for solo and orchestra without the traditional 'tutti' would have been almost cried down. And yet we have lived to see this strong tradition broken through.

Mendelssohn did this at a stroke in his first concerto, in G minor. He set aside the first conventional 'tutti', & using only a few introductory bars for the orchestra dashed at once into his solo. In a still more forcible and precise [manner] has he commenced his only violin concerto. But in this work, notwithstanding the absence of the introductory 'tutti', the orchestra is fully and actively employed, always giving relief & imagination to the work.

Carl Maria v. Weber must not be forgotten in referring to the above important subject. Although he wrote concertos on the accepted plan of the day, one cannot fail to see a desire to escape the form in that beautiful composition of his, the 'Concertstück'.

Whatever the future may decide as to the plan or form upon which a concerto should be written, one thing is certain: that the great men of the past who have given us these works, whether with 'tutti' or without 'tutti', will never be forgotten. Only the inferior imitators of that which they cannot feel will sink into obscurity.

One branch of music I scarcely venture to remark upon. It is a branch which must be appreciated with great care & reverence and have no words lightly applied to it. I mean 'church music'.

In speaking of particular forms of composition & their hold on the public when once accepted it would be unjust not to mention the deep-rooted affection which the public has for the works of old cathedral composers. They have long enjoyed a well deserved immunity from invasion. How long this security is to be accorded to them I will not undertake to prophesy; signs indeed are appearing that melody will make its way, side by side with mastery, & perhaps old established form or fashion must give way.

'Fashion' in performance[1]

A few words might be said upon fashion in performance, whether vocal or instrumental. The change in performance <of the present day> has been more gradual and more traceable than the change in composition. Let us take the pianoforte as the most universally used instrument. But how has it changed its character in the last thirty or forty years! – more keys, thicker strings (therefore having more resistance), inducing, if I may use the expression, harder playing. And yet it is a great question whether the public really get more enjoyment of the instrument than [in] the days of Clementi, Cramer, & Dussek. With the piano of their time, they learn[ed] to draw out the tone in a tender manner, as was taught to them by their early studies on the harpsichord.

Conclusion

I have endeavoured to show the influence which the art-fashion has had on music, to show how deeply rooted is every manner when once accepted. It takes a generation to mould a manner, and an equal time at least to set it aside. The great men are those who study closely the art as it stands and see an opening by which they can improve upon the model. One thing seems certain: that all those who have been successful in breaking through the barriers have themselves studied upon the form of their predecessors. Their very originality is the result of this course.

Let me quote a few words from the 'Discourses of Sir Joshua Reynolds'. He says: 'I know there are many artists of great fame who appear never to have looked out of themselves, and who probably would think it derogatory to their character, to be supposed to borrow from any other painter. But when we recollect and compare the works of such men with those who took to their assistance the inventions of others we shall be convinced of the great advantage of the latter practice.' Again, says Sir Joshua, 'The daily food and nourishment of the mind of an artist is found in the works of his predecessors. There is no other way for him to become great himself.'[2] I quote these words from so great a master as a safeguard against any remarks I may have imperfectly made upon new impending forms in music.

1 This brief section was evidently inserted as an afterthought. It is written on a facing page, and in a much more hurried hand than the 'fair copy' style of the main text.

2 Quoted from Reynolds, *Discourses*, 208, 211–12.

To very few indeed has it been ordained that they should shape the art anew. Those who have ever done it, always in a very palpable manner evince their respect and gratitude for what has gone before.

Let me then say that the student in music should never lose sight of the whole history & tradition of his art. When he has become a thorough master, and I may say almost an intimate acquaintance of the composers of past times, then, & then only if he be endowed with genius, can he hope to give us a step onwards into some design to help music.

One cannot believe that any composer, ever so gifted, really of his own will dashed into a new school.

In the transition of art many flakes & atoms are flying about seeking for a resting place and a guiding spirit. Such guides are not to be found every day, such as Alessandro Scarlatti, Bach, Handel, Gluck, Haydn – and (the name may sound strange) Rossini.

Beethoven, {Mozart,} Weber, & Mendelssohn have places assigned to them in the history of music which will remain to them as long as the art exists.[1]

Let me then urge students in music of the present day not only to be diligent but to be thoughtful, not looking to immediate reward but giving patient study to the rich bequests of past times. Perhaps in 50 years or in a century the 'art-fashion' of our day will be open to the same criticism as we are now applying to the past. It will be said of us that our instrumental pieces were nearly an hour long, and that in England we were not content with one {such} specimen in a concert but generally three or four; that our concerts lasted often more than three hours and operas nearly four, and that beginning the entertainments [sic] at a late hour they were not finished until midnight.

That gatherings of 4 thousand performers for the purpose of giving sacred music frequently took place[2] but those who expected a finished exhibition were under the circumstances often disappointed. That the English were known to be fond of the best music, and to spend large sums of money on it.

Notwithstanding all this it will be said that we were also much taken up at this period with a certain class of composition called a ballad (totally unlike the ballad of still earlier times) and that we went so far as to sit out a concert with no other kind of performance but these ballads (pretty as many of them were) from beginning to end.[3]

1 By inference, Bennett conveys the idea that the composers in the second list, however great, were not 'guides' or innovators like those in the first list. He had said as much more clearly in his earlier lecture on 'Music of the Present Time': see above, p. 135, though with slightly different lists of names.

2 This refers no doubt to the Handel performances at the Crystal Palace.

3 Ballad concerts were organised by publishers to promote the sale of sheet music. One

Such a chronicle would not be untruthful – neither would it be discreditable to the musical world as it now stands, nor to England. Germany might share with us in the complaints a descendant would make as to the length of instrumental compositions. In the length of our performances they would have nothing to do with us.[1] Germany naturally looks with a surprise akin to horror upon our long programmes, wondering how an audience can be found to sit them out patiently – and, more important, still wonders [that] such a heavy report can be duly prepared for the guests.[2]

Nevertheless reward will not be wanting to those nations which have worked hard in the cause. Germany will be pointed to as having produced in this generation very splendid editions of the classical masters, recalling the time when old Walsh of Catherine Street produced the copper plate editions of Händel.

England may justly claim at this time to have sent into every body's hand the cheapest book of the classics in music which any country in Europe is able to produce.[3] May the publishers of the future when they are poring over the history of music, as exemplified in our time, not overlook the zeal & enterprise (prompted by the innate taste of the public) with which the so-called merchants of music have supplied our daily musical wants.

There is now little or no excuse for a student not becoming acquainted with the whole range of the art; and speaking for England, I sincerely trust that all our young people will work for its reputation and produce specimens of music which may encourage the hope that in any new state of things we may take a part.[4]

series was given at St. James's Hall by Boosey & Co. in the early 1860s (Simpson, *A Century of Ballads*, 212–13). The term 'ballad concert' seems to have been first used for a concert given by Charlotte Sainton-Dolby on 3 January 1866 under the management of Chappell & Co. (Scholes, *Mirror*, 293).

1 The meaning of these two sentences is not immediately clear. Bennett seems to be saying that while future historians might criticise Germany for the length of individual instrumental compositions, Britain would be much more likely to be censured for the length of its concert programmes.

2 The analytical programme note was a peculiarly English phenomenon, and was observed (generally with admiration) by several foreign visitors. See Bashford, 'Not just "G." ', 118–19.

3 Bennett is perhaps thinking primarily of the vocal scores of choral works published by J. Alfred Novello, which caused a drastic reduction in price that was a boon to choral societies. See Krummel, 'Music Publishing', 57–8.

4 The final paragraph appears to be a late addition to the fair copy of the main text.

11

Bach and Handel

Arts School, Cambridge, 4 February 1871

One thing that first arrests our attention in reviewing the history of modern music is its very rapid development within the last two centuries, and the small number of great master minds employed in that development. Whatever progress music may have made during the middle ages is a question, it may be, of deep interest to the musical historian. There is no doubt, however, that the works with which the musician has chiefly to do were all written in one short epoch of the world's history, in which a few great masters follow so closely upon each other, that there is never a link missing in that brilliant chain, and each one increased tenfold the profits of his predecessors' labours.

One of the results of our great masters' living in point of time so closely together is that unless we look closely into dates, we are always apt to consider them too much as contemporaries, and forgetting the influence which the mere progress of time had on the progress of art, to draw comparisons between the contributions of each {of them} to the art.

The fact that these great musicians lived almost within the memory of man & of our having every source of information respecting them easily open to us, the ease also with which any one can collect all the works of these masters – these circumstances aid us in drawing comparisons between their achievements; and the very fact of discovering in our researches how nearly equal was their genius, and how difficult it would be to show which had done most for music, gives an interest & a weight to that question so often asked (& often rashly answered): which of the great musicians was the greatest? But as there seems nothing to gain by a decision concerning the relative greatness of these masters, so discussions of such a question are apt to lead to much prejudice, to partisanship hastily formed on a hollow basis and productive of dire results to him who attends to them.

Let him who neglects to study the works of one of these great masters, because he has heard that there is a greater musician who merits more of his attention – let him, I say, look into the lives of the men whose qualities he is discussing and see what they thought of one another, and then I think he will agree with me that it is more profitable to regard them as fellow workers, each with his special work done by himself alone, and done so perfectly that the word 'superiority' becomes altogether inapplicable.

We seem to lose the best effect which music can have upon us if we attempt to look upon the results of those great men's labours as anything but an harmonious whole, for we shall never find in one of them any thing which will compensate for the ignorance of the works of another. They must be studied all together if we wish to have the idea of the art in its perfect state for which each one of them was working.

I have touched upon this subject because I do not wish, in any comparisons to which this lecture may give rise, to be thought to compare the relative greatness of our great masters.

Let us not make rivals of those who looked upon each other in no other light than as fellow workers, not only having the same object, but having at the same time the consciousness that that object could not be effected without the assistance of others. And remember if in the history of music we find great musicians with what are called rivals, those rivals are always persons of a very inferior order of merit, never those of an equal order of merit with themselves.

Now in comparing the works of these great composers, we may try to find out how much of the result is due to the individual characteristics of the composers, how much is due to any external circumstances which may have influenced them, and how much in the works of a particular writer is due to the works of his predecessor. If then we select two composers at random, our comparisons would be much impeded by our having constantly to consider the difference of materials with which they worked; but if we can find two great masters exactly contemporaneous, we shall know that they enjoyed the same legacies from their forerunners, & if we find that these two masters lived under very different circumstances and with many opposite influences acting upon them we shall be able to trace the effect which such influence may have had on their careers.

I propose then by a <comparison>{short review} of the lives & works of Handel & Bach to point out the special characteristics of each of these composers, and to show at the same time, as far as possible, the influence which the external circumstances in which they lived had upon their works. These great men were sent to us about the same time, born within one year of each other and living almost to the same age – both Germans. They were the greatest masters of the art in a technical point of view that ever lived; neither before nor since has any composer approached them. Bach always, Handel towards the later part of his life, adopted the highest form of composition. These are some of the reasons which lead us to think of these men almost as twins – but in reality they had little in common, save that which they had in common with every body else. Hence no comparison ought to be drawn between them as to their relative merits, but a close examination of their works & style will always be of the utmost value to the student in music.

In this country we know more of Handel than of Bach; in Germany, if I am not greatly in error, they know much less of Handel than we do. Handel for many years adopted England as his home. Bach never left Germany, and his works have but slowly made their way to us. While Handel's works were published in an expensive edition during his life time by an English publisher, Bach was engaged with his sons, either in transcribing or himself engraving his compositions. The industry of these two men must have been enormous.

In the case of Bach we have indeed but recently received fresh evidence through the splendid Leipzig edition of his works, which appear with such regularity & care that one might believe the composer to be alive to superintend the issue.[1]

Most musical students know that every week a new composition by him was sung in the Thomas Church at Leipzig consecutively for four years, and these compositions form a very rich collection of church music; but few were aware of the vast store of instrumental works which he left us & which are now appearing. His compositions for the organ, his concertos for one, two, three, and four harpsichords, with orchestral accompaniments, {violin concertos} and a hundred other productions, a simple catalogue of which is sufficient to excite astonishment, would still be unknown if it were not for the edition of his works now appearing.

Handel's industry and facility astonish all who think of the matter. Having for years endured all the turmoils of theatrical management; constantly producing for his theatre in the Haymarket Italian operas with varying success – many of which are now almost forgotten; losing a large fortune, having to bear with the caprices of his singers; yet he never lost his power, and even under these difficulties, commenced late in life those sublime works but for which he might have remained comparatively unknown. One fact, a fact which is scarcely credible, I must mention here, viz. that the 'Messiah', of which I intend to speak more fully presently, was composed in the short space of three weeks – and this statement is attested in the manuscript score at Buckingham Palace; and

1 By 1871 the *Bachgesellschaft* had published nineteen volumes of Bach's music.

'Israel in Egypt' in a very little longer time. What an example of his indomitable energy & industry.

There is no doubt, as I have said before, that external circumstances influenced the style of their compositions. In the music of Handel we see the man of the world, one who thoroughly knows his own worth, has constantly watched the verdict of the public (no bad test after all), and educated himself into a broad & massive view of what music should be to lay hold of a public. On the other hand we see in the music of Bach the work of a devoted and conscientious recluse, who cared not for the large public, but rather coveted the satisfaction of his children <(all musical)> and his immediate friends.

It would be impossible for me to pretend on this occasion to make an analysis of the numberless works of Bach & Handel. My wish is to confine myself to pointing out the leading principles which these great men adopted in their work, and their general style of manipulation; and I sincerely trust that when my remarks are finished no one will be able to tell which composer excites my greatest admiration, or to suppose that any rivalship could possibly exist between such ardent fellow-workers in the cause of art.

Side by side with that sublime work 'the Messiah,' I will place a work now fortunately becoming known to us in England, the Passions Musik of Bach.[1] After that I will point to other classes of composition of these authors.

Perhaps with regard to this work of Bach, as it is so little known, it would not be improper for me to say something of its history.[2] After Bach's death all his works passed into the libraries of S. Thomas at Leipsic, of the Orphan Asylum at Berlin, and of different private individuals, where they lay covered with dust for the space of nearly a century. At length discovery was made at Berlin of a work for two choirs with full orchestral accompaniments.[3] This was the Passions Musik. It was executed through the zeal of Mendelssohn at Berlin, and its beauties proved that great as was the reputation of the old master already, not half of his merits were known. Of the history of the Messiah it is unnecessary to speak in this place.

1 The *St. Matthew Passion*. Bennett had directed the first British performance of this work, presented by the Bach Society on 6 April 1854 (Bennett, *Life*, 234).

2 The original word, instead of 'history', was 'discovery' (in the rough draft).

3 The rough draft of the lecture has: 'At length discovery was made of a mass in B. Minor for two choirs with full orchestral accompaniments, this was the Passions Musik the beauties of which proved that great as his reputation was already not half of his merits were known.' It is hardly conceivable that Bennett, who had directed at least two performances of the *St. Matthew Passion*, can have failed to distinguish the two works, and this must have been a momentary confusion.

Now to return to the contrast of the two works. With regard to 'the Messiah' there is no doubt that Handel, either through his librettist or through extreme haste, suffered the plan of his work to be rendered in a confused form. It may indeed be said that the work in any case would suffer from over richness and from the multitude of its enchanting themes and imposing choruses. But the point upon which I have the temerity to tread lies in another direction. The plan of the 'Passions-Musik' & even of 'the Elijah' (to speak of modern times) cannot allow a single number to be omitted; and yet one can scarcely tell in the Messiah what pieces are to be omitted or included.[1] But there is strong evidence of such practices in the life-time of Handel himself. He appears not to have been scrupulous as to the omission, the substitution or addition of pieces to please the public for the moment, or satisfy the wants of some particular occasion.

I may here allude to a curious fact. On looking back to one of Handel's earliest and most beautiful works, although not one of his grandest – the 'Acis & Galatea' – there will be found in the original M. S. a supplementary chorus in which 'Acis', having previously been killed by Polyphemus, is now taking a principal part. This chorus I have not heard, although it was printed under my direction after I had inspected the original score for the purpose of bringing out a new edition of the work under the auspices of the English Handel Society;[2] nor do I believe it has ever been performed in modern times.

In certain parts of the Messiah it is difficult to follow out the idea with which the composer has been working. Nothing can be more beautiful, in an artistic sense, than the commencement of the oratorio, and indeed throughout the whole of the first part – but in the second part at the commencement, where the sublime chorus 'Behold the Lamb of God' is followed by the equally sublime song 'He was despised,' one fails to see in a musical sense the natural connection onwards to the chorus 'Surely he hath borne our griefs' which is placed in a key having little or no affinity to what has gone before; and the two magnificent choruses mentioned seem to knock against and injure each other, being so near

1 In Handel's defence it should be said that *Messiah*, unlike the other two works mentioned, has no dramatic story line and therefore could be (and was) reordered by the composer without structural damage.

2 Bennett's edition of *Acis and Galatea* appeared in 1847 as the seventh volume of *The Works of Handel*, published by Cramer, Beale & Co. for the English Handel Society. The chorus referred to, 'Smiling Venus', had never been published. Bennett found it bound into the autograph (British Library R.M.20.a.2). Handel had used it for the first time in the bilingual 'Serenata' version of the work produced at the King's Theatre in 1732: see Smith, *Concerning Handel*, 216–19, and Dean, *Handel's Dramatic Oratorios*, 174, 183. The scenario of that production has not been fully reconstructed.

together. In other works of Handel similar instances may be found, which seems to show that he consulted rather the grand power he possessed in placing any number of rich choruses before the public than of attending closely to dramatic construction. The 'Hallelujah' chorus in the Messiah, one of the greatest pieces of music ever written, judged from whatever point of view, certainly takes away from the effect of the final choruses in the same key.

But what composer can we name, not even Bach, who brings so much power & majesty to bear upon the art which he loved & elevated? Not even that commercial principle which he is known to have cultivated could destroy or even injure that lofty view which he took of the gifts with which he was endowed. Throughout all circumstances, whether of comparative adversity or ruffle of temper caused by those of his craft with whom he had to deal, he never lost sight of the great mission he had to perform, whether in his native country or in Italy, or in London.

He has enriched most branches of the art. His operas may not be remembered in their entirety, but many beautiful things from them will always find a place. His clavier music (published under a patent from George the 2nd in London) will always give delight to the student. His many other instrumental works, such as organ & oboe concertos, trios for stringed instruments, overtures to his many operas, can never be stamped out.

{Now back to Bach again.} It is time we gave new ears to music in the shape of John Sebastian Bach. If you expect to find the power & effect of Handel in the works of Bach you will be disappointed; but for mastery in the science & in tenderness of detail he has never been surpassed & in my opinion never will be. Let any musical student study the first bar of his Passions Musik & see how much more he was devoted to his innate feeling for the art than he was to the applause of the multitude. Here he seems to draw from musical thinkers what Handel seems to command. In point of colossal form, the Passions Musik will not compare with the oratorios of Handel, but as regards watchfulness of detail no master that we know can take Bach's place.

This lovely & truly the most sacred work ever written will soon make its way with us, and we shall sing it every last term, as they do at Leipzig. From the beginning to the end no word of the severest critic can come upon it. It is a work which its composer did not let loose from his hands until he was most thoroughly satisfied. He wanted no librettist;[1] he took the text of the 26th chapter of St. Matthew and bestowed all his care & great power upon it. Look to the force of Bach's dramatic power in this

[1] This is of course untrue. The librettist for the Passion was 'Picander' (Christian Friedrich Henrici).

modest but great work. Let the student examine this composition and see what master ever excelled in 'finish' what Bach has shown us. But not only in 'finish' does Bach show his power; he shows that he can compete with any composer who ever lived (not even excepting Handel) in touching the feelings of those in the world who have any ear for music, and even in arousing an audience to his mastery, although he probably never had his reward in this respect and never expected it.

I have already spoken of the first bar of his wonderful work the Passions Musik. Every bar is worthy of consideration & study to the musical student, indeed I may say every note, for to me never did a note seem to be out of its place. Another equally beautiful work, wrought with the same modesty & conscience, is the Passions-Musik according to the text of St. John. This work should be studied by all who wish to become acquainted with the characteristics of Bach.

One other subject I must slightly allude to here, though at some future time I purpose to bring these two great men before you separately. There is evidence in favour of Bach being by far the greatest performer on the organ & harpsichord. Handel had no organ in London at all to compare with Bach's at Leipzig, nor does it appear that he wrote anything in the shape of the splendid & superb music with pedal obligato bequeathed to organists by Bach.[1] Bach's clavier-musik is also a rich collection, throwing into the shade [in] a numerical sense the harpsichord lessons of Handel. Bach even essayed the sonata form, as witness the opening movement of the 'Suites Anglaises', no approach to such a form being found in Handel.[2] I wish my remarks on this last subject to be taken as quite introductory, for as I said before I intend to bring these men before you separately as regards their numerous other claims to your compositions [sic].

And in conclusion, may we not reflect upon the state in which the art would have been at the present time had not these giants been sent to us[?] Who can calculate the influence of their work & their example? Perhaps the easiest reckoning would be for us to consider in what state music would be at the present time if Bach & Handel were swept away altogether and that we were never to hear another note belonging to either. Some of the old masters would still be left us, but with works (as beautiful as they are) in many respects so limited in their plan that people with ideas of music would feel they had no basis for their study. Would not young musicians impetuously rush to make a reputation in

1 Pedals were virtually unknown on English organs in Handel's day.

2 It is difficult to detect a precursor of 'sonata form' in the opening movement of English Suite No. 1. Handel, on the other hand, came very close to it in several pieces, such as the Fantasia in C (HWV 490).

the art they have taken up, but for the 'Israel in Egypt', 'Judas Maccabeus', the Messiah, the Passions-Musik, the Xmas Oratorio and other achievements <raising their hands before them, telling them to study the art with industry & entire devotion> {standing before them as examples} [?][1]

[1] Bennett evidently had some trouble deciding how to end this lecture.

12

Mozart

Arts School, Cambridge, 4 March 1871

As I have said in a former lecture,[1] never was there a period in the history of music so fraught with anxiety and deep interest as that of the present. Never was there a time when it was more necessary for those studying music with a view to obtain any eminence in the art to look about them closely and thoughtfully and see what is going on at this moment.

Let them watch on the indications (clear to a practised eye) which point to the unsettled state of the art. I use the term 'unsettled' in no desponding spirit, for music has had its revolutions like nations, and according to our knowledge has {chiefly} been the gainer. Whether every succeeding revolution is to be a success and lead to a further development of the art on ground principles is a question which few would have courage enough to answer.

In the present day there is much of composition in all styles – good, indifferent, and bad for a young musician to study. It will be for him to choose his path and shape his taste – and a very perilous matter is this decision. Certainly, very few of our greatest musicians have been without the guidance of experienced teachers, these being their immediate predecessors; but teaching is only part of the matter; it is the self-control and patient study of the young artist which will effect the bulk of his success. His difficulty will lie between pedantry and scholarship, between wild enthusiasm and absolute tameness.

Again it is reasonable to suppose that a young artist has a favorite author of whom he is continually thinking, and whose works continually possess him. As the favorite composer will probably be chosen on account of some striking and special quality in his works, this matter

1 This refers to the lecture 'Music in the Present Time': see above, p. 129.

must appear very serious. The student would but freely imitate any striking point and risk the chance of [not?] learning outline and form.

It would be better to work upon the model of a so-called dry composer who knew form, than to run this 'wild goose chase'. But there is little need to be brought down to the study of the works of a dry composer. Let the history of music be well studied, and as the art now stands, it goes over no great length of time; let a young artist begin in instrumental music from the time of Haydn down to the time of Mendelssohn; let him watch closely and thoughtfully the characteristics of each composer who wrote in between the time of the two great men I have mentioned; let him also, as far as possible, become acquainted with their <habits> {plan} of work, the circumstances under which they worked, nay even (it is not to be left out of consideration) under what domestic or worldly influence they pursued their artistic life. Beyond these enquiries, let a student find out the taste and requirements of the public at the time in which each master wrote, and endeavour to find out how much each composer resisted or yielded to the demands of the <public> world. Such researches as I now suggest would, I believe, be of the utmost importance in forming the character of one entering the study of music.

In former lectures of mine, here, you will perhaps have observed that I avoided giving you any biographical information as to composers, for in the present day nearly every musician of mark has one or more volumes appropriated to his works and doings.

It would only be fair for me at this moment to admit that in limiting the time of our enquiry as to the state of 'music and musicians' from the time of Haydn to Mendelssohn, I have been thinking more of modern instrumental music and music for the modern theatre <than of any other music>. I shall not be accused of ignoring the claims of Handel, Bach and Gluck by those who have attended in this room before – but as I said on the last occasion of being here, the art which chiefly supplies our concert rooms and theatres at the present day is comparatively new. Handel still survives at Birmingham and Exeter Hall[1] in majestic power – and will assert himself as long as the art exists. Let us hope that his great contemporary John Sebastian Bach will be equally at home with us very soon.

When I say that the form of art upon which we now exist is comparatively new, I do not exceed the truth. Let me say for example that I have held long conversations upon Haydn, his works, and his personal manners with one who knew and recollected him well[2] – also, (going

[1] That is, the Birmingham Triennial Music Festival, and the concerts of the Sacred Harmonic Society at Exeter Hall, London. See pp. 32, 37.

[2] Probably William Crotch, who taught Bennett composition at the Royal Academy of Music in 1831 (Bennett, *Life*, 21). Crotch had performed to Haydn at Oxford in 1791 and met him over dinner (Rennert, *Crotch*, 34). Another link was Sir George Smart (see p. 118).

back a little farther than I ought to do according to my plan) I have conversed with a musician, who in a conversation with me when I was a student upon musical matters, referred to Charles Philip Emmanuel Bach as his 'dear friend'.[1] <Certain it is that many are now alive who knew Beethoven> Also many interesting conversations have I had with a very dear old friend of mine, the late Thomas Attwood, one of the most genial musicians who ever lived, upon his master Mozart. Dussek is still remembered by a few —Spohr, Weber, Meyerbeer, Mendelssohn are quite within the memory of the present generation.

So then, I speak of music as almost a new art – the range of which is not too wide for any student at all anxious to make himself acquainted with the principles upon which he should study.

And now for the way of study, and who is to be model!

As I have said, more than once, it is not necessary that the most dashing and brilliant genius that ever appeared should be your model; indeed I believe that such a model would be a dangerous guide. I have also told you that you will find models of highly accomplished scholarship <without the term 'dry' being applied to them> {combined with genius}, and one of these you must seek.

Who shall it be?

But before I enter farther into this very tender point, let me beg of you not to misunderstand me in any remarks I may have to make in regards to those great men whose names I must presently mention. I shall, I trust, treat their positions in the art with due reverence – and if I (in my own opinion only) give preference to one over another, upon the particular point under review (namely the selection of a model), remember that I, according to my duty, have an equal regard for them all – and that no man who ever practised music as a profession can be more annoyed than I am when I hear great masters compared. Their styles may be compared, but not their reputations.

Let me suppose a conclave or committee of young artists in music, discussing the question as to what composer and his works they would adopt. It must be assumed that students who enter into this discussion have mastered the elementary part of the art – that they can write mechanical exercises with fluency, can read the scores of great masters placed in their hands, want no instrument (such as the pianoforte) to help them in the realisation of the master's productions. Let me then, I say, suppose one of this enthusiastic body of young musicians to rise and propose one man who should be the model upon which they should work.

Shall it first be Joseph Haydn, one of the greatest benefactors to

1 This informant is unidentified.

music, who wrote 118 symphonies, about 83 quartetts for stringed instrument, many operas unfortunately lost, a rich collection of pianoforte music, and sacred works treasured within ourselves?

Shall it be Cherubini, to whom we [are] indebted in many directions, not the least of which is the brilliancy of his instrumentation and minute marking of expression in orchestral works?

Would it be Beethoven? Many votes would of a certainty be given to this proposition, for a grander name has never been inserted in the list of truly great men.

Would it be Weber? for who has so well described himself in indelible letters as a genius.

Shall it be Spohr? the last to depart from us, among the great masters.[1]

Shall it be Meyerbeer? who brought dramatic power & effect into the theatre unknown to the time before him.

Shall it be Rossini? who took hold of the music of the theatre at a grasp.

Shall it be Mendelssohn? who has contributed such glorious and finished masterpieces to the art, in all directions.

I might go further and ask shall it be Schumann or Wagner but that my plan has decided the limit.

But I will not keep you longer waiting for my opinion – and will narrow the question to two men – Haydn & Mozart.

They were strangely mixed up together. Haydn came first and stayed last. Without doubt he was the originator of the present form of instrumental music, but Mozart instantly seized it, made grand work of it, and the result was that Haydn enlarged his symphonies (as shown in the 12 grand composed for England) after the manner of Mozart.

All things considered I cannot longer hesitate as to the one I should place before you for your study and guidance, and therefore I name Mozart.

Let us briefly consider the claims which Mozart has upon us to be placed in this position. I shall not give you a catalogue of his works, but refer chiefly to his characteristics as a composer, the first among them being his <u>thorough earnestness</u>, and <u>deep thought</u>, exhibited in all his music whether of one class or another. This quality it is open to every student to imitate; not so, those beautiful themes & melodies now the property of the world through his inspiration – this is impossible. But far inferior musicians to Mozart have been similarly gifted.

Another immensely strong claim Mozart makes upon your attention

[1] Note that this remark can be interpreted to imply that no great master was still living in 1871, and that Meyerbeer, Rossini, Berlioz, Liszt, Wagner and Verdi fell short of the status of 'great master', for they all outlived Spohr, who died in 1859.

and study, and that is in broad rhythm, which few composers can manage with complete success. I know of no composer, with perhaps the exception of Beethoven, who gives us such specimens of the real 'Adagio'. Take for instance the Adagio from the Stringed Quintett in G Minor [K.516]; a small sonata in E flat [K.282], beginning with such a movement and ending with a minuet; take an adagio in B minor for the pianoforte [K.540], published separately; study the 13 concert arias, a work sufficient to make the reputation of any man.

Above all, study his symphonies and his operas. Remember how much we owe to him for not only enlarging instrumental music, but for placing opera in that dignified position for which {, it must be admitted,} Gluck had prepared it. Idomeneo was written at the age of twenty five, and it has been well said that youthful fire was never so happily tempered with experience. This was to be expected from one who could write an opera like the 'Seraglio' at the age of 14.[1] Also let it not be forgotten that Mozart did more for pianoforte music on a large scale than any one who came before him; no further proof is wanting than to look at his more than twenty concertos for the pianoforte and orchestra.

It is said of Mozart in connection with P[iano] Forte music that he was the first to suggest the idea of duett playing on the pianoforte – of course, the duetts we now see of the music of Bach and Handel are mere arrangements. Referring to these duetts of Mozart, there is a work, in two or more numbers, originally written for a musical clock [K.516f], but afterwards no doubt applied by himself to the pianoforte. This work gives you the very essence of music.

Another very great claim which Mozart has upon the admiration of young musicians is the esteem and devotion he exhibited towards other artists. Take, for instance, the accompaniments to the 'Messiah' which will for ever associate his name with that of Handel; and yet at the time he could not have divined how necessary would such accompaniments be, when performers entered on a larger scale.

The players of stringed instruments will also be grateful to Mozart for his contribution towards their department in the shape of twelve quartetts – and those magnificent quintetts – all written in <u>his profoundest manner</u>. Also did Mozart like to look back upon the art of past time, and give striking examples, in no caricature spirit, of his admiration and appreciation of it – witness his introduction and fugue in the style of 'G. F. Handel' [K.546]. One can see at a glance that this is not a joke, but a trial of skill, with one of his great predecessors.

But <u>hundreds</u> of other instances could be shown to exemplify the

[1] This is inaccurate, of course. *Die Entführung aus dem Serail* dates from 1782, when Mozart was 26.

extreme devotion and love which Mozart had for the art. In one sense, he seems to stand alone. While other great musicians have had the finest immediate instruction which could be found, Mozart appears to have done everything for himself from his boyhood, save the scanty help afforded him by his father, a musician of very small power, and which help need scarcely be taken into account.

{'His conscience was his muse.' He seems never to have made a mistake. If anything could possibly be laid to his charge, it would be that he was ever serious and possibly too much so in certain phases of the art.}

Conclusion

In bringing the name of Mozart so prominently before you this morning, I shall have placed myself in a very false position, if you at all understand me [to say] that your attention and study is to be <altogether> diverted from other masters who have 'a thousand and one' claims upon your gratitude.

In choosing Mozart as your study, I touch a point in musical history at which a very complete review of the art can be taken from the earliest time to the latest. I have not told you that Mozart was the greatest composer of his time, or of any time. Also, I believe, I have not confounded a man of genius with a consummate master, although there are to be found those in whom the characters are combined – great men indeed! and Mozart was one of them.

In making my choice of Mozart as a true model of conscience and mastery, and suggesting such a model to you, I am not speaking at random. It is the deep conviction resulting from a careful study of all the characteristics, temperaments, habits of working, self denial of public applause, commercial gain, hasty ambition, and many other conflicting influences to be found in the history of great musicians.

Mozart was not over-burdened with the smiles of fortune, but always true to the letter in his art. What did he say to a publisher who once advised him to write in a more popular style, otherwise he could not continue to purchase his compositions? 'Then I can make no more by my pen, and I had better starve, and go to destruction at once.'

This was the answer of the genuine artist; and most truly did he ever in his works show that he cared nothing for present gain, and would be content that posterity should care for his reputation – which indeed, it is hoped they will do, in spite of the vague and eccentric attractions put forth by many composers of the present day, which bewilder the public, and which almost lead them to think that the state of art in the Mozart period is inadequate to the wants of the present day.

It is indeed to be deplored that with the march of events in music, with large and enthusiastic bodies of amateurs never content save in organising large orchestras and choruses, that [the] delicate, beautiful, and highly finished works of Mozart should be heard only at intervals. So with the works of Haydn. But it cannot be believed that even a partial neglect of such masterpieces can permanently be allowed.

It may perhaps be suggested that young and small societies should be formed for the purpose of constantly performing such works as those I am now mentioning. But young and small societies are more ambitious than old societies. The promoters of young societies are anxious to show to the public that they are alive to what is called the onward progress of the art. I cannot sympathise with this feeling. Perhaps I am too conservative, but at any rate I can point to an old saying 'We must walk before can run', and to walk in the way of Mozart would ensure a pretty quick and firm step in the afterlife of an artist.

Is the present growth of orchestras to put aside the masterpieces of Haydn & Mozart, because many of the instruments now enjoyed can find no employment [in them]? Should it not rather be a matter of wonder that so much real force and sound come out of the composition of these men with the limited means at their disposal? And ought not a young student to note the fact that the superabundant means of brass instruments used in the present day often serve as a disguise to the 'slippy' (if I may use such a term) manner, in which the [deficient] four-part writing of the stringed instrument[s] too often shows when we are allowed to examine the score[?]

Can such a neglect for the true principles of composition be found in the works of Haydn and Mozart[?] Never! The true balance of power in orchestras was much better known to them than by many composers of the present day. Ask all violin players and other members of the family of stringed instruments, and they will tell you what they think of this question. With all their delicacy of bowing, with all care of intonation, with all the precision, special to their department, they will confess, or rather complain, that the unmeaning use of instruments up above[1] in the orchestra mar[s] their efforts.

Mozart never allowed this to be the case; neither did Haydn. They certainly knew the use of trumpets, horns and drums – but they treated them as gentlemen, not as brigands. Mozart even used trombones, but only in certain situations requiring a peculiar effect – instance the 'statue scene' in 'Don Giovanni'.

Let me not get into a dissertation upon instrumentation; there is

[1] Orchestras were often arrayed on raked concert platforms in which the brass and percussion instruments were placed on a higher level than the strings, as is often the case today.

plenty enough to talk about in this subject, if taken by itself. My object in going even so far is to show you the great power which {such a man as} Mozart possessed, and which was tempered by that modesty & veneration which he knew must be associated with the canons of his art.

As great a man we may possibly see again; a greater man, viewed as a consummate master – never!

I have said in the early part of my lecture that I intentionally abstained from giving you facts and scraps which can [be] gathered by yourselves from biographies. Just as I am closing, I may say that there is one book which must always ensure credit to England for having produced it. This is the life of Mozart by Edward Holmes – a professor of music of sterling reputation, although little known to the world outside.

The <impressions> {copies} of this book are now scarce, but it was the first biography worth any notice. It is now probably translated into Mozart's mother-tongue,[1] and thus the Germans will know through the medium of an Englishman how keenly alive we are (cold, as we are often represented) to the real men of art.

{He [Mozart] himself kept a register (afterwards published) of the date and appearance of his works. He seemed to have done himself no justice in the matter.}[2]

[1] No German edition of Holmes's *Life of Mozart* has been traced.

[2] The text ends here. Evidently the closing sentences of the lecture have been lost, or perhaps were never written out.

Appendix

Music for the Sheffield Lectures

In April 1859 Bennett delivered two lectures to the Sheffield Literary and Philosophical Society. Their titles and printed syllabuses were essentially the same as Lectures 1 and 2 delivered to the London Institution the previous year, and he evidently used the same manuscript text, revising it in some cases to suit the new situation. The more significant revisions have been noted in footnotes to Lectures 1 and 2.

The concert at the end of the first lecture, however, was quite different from the one given in London, chiefly no doubt because a different set of performers was available. Moreover Bennett now provided programme notes. The illustrative music for the second Sheffield lecture was interspersed in the text, as in London, but most of the pieces were different.

First Sheffield Lecture

27 April 1859
Concert Programme, with Notes

Pianoforte,
Professor W. S. Bennett, and Mr. Percival Phillips,
with vocal performers

Harpsichord Lessons	Scarlatti, Handel
Fugue	J. Seb. Bach

The harpsichord music of Scarlatti, Bach & Handel must be reckoned amongst the most learned music extant, but its learning is even exceeded by the poetic fancy which it developed. Let it however be remembered that no Broadwood pianoforte existed at the time of Handel & Scarlatti, and that the absence of sustaining power in the instruments then in vogue led to the adoption of a style of passage which has been [in] a measure superseded by subsequent composers. Nevertheless the beauty of the harmonical progression in these now ancient compositions has not been improved upon, and whilst the art remains these remarkable pieces must survive. I do not recommend these pieces as introductory to later masters; they must be taken in hand when the pupil is materially advanced.

Symphony (Duet)	Haydn

The Symphony of Haydn, which with the assistance of Mr. Percival Phillips I will now present to you, is one of the twelve [']grand['] written for Salomon's concerts in London. It is remarkable for its lovely themes and their admirable development. Indeed to Haydn belongs the title of 'Father of Instrumental Music', for to him are we entirely indebted for a new form of composition. He had previously written upwards of a hundred symphonies and 80 quartetts before he undertook to write the twelve grand symphonies for Salomon.

Song, 'Ere Infancy's Bud'[1]	Méhul

The composer of the next piece in my selection was an elegant French musician, pupil of Gluck and composer of the oratorio of Joseph, from which you are about to hear a specimen. He is a master, who with later composers, such as Boieldieu & Auber, has done the greatest honour to the French school.

Air and Variations, P. F.	Mozart

With regard to Mozart it is not necessary {I am sure} for me to advocate his claims before you, but I am anxious to draw your attention to the fact that there is a large amount of <pianoforte> {chamber} music made purposely for home enjoyment, for instance his many pianoforte {solo} sonatas, also those with violin accompaniment, his trios & quartets, airs & var[iatio]ns &c, not forgetting his smaller vocal pieces, by which I mean those not belonging to his magnificent operas. I should not leave this pleasant theme so quickly were it not that I hope to refer largely to it in my lecture on Friday evening next.

Song, 'Where the primrose'[2]	Arne

From the death of Purcell to that of Arne, a period of more than fourscore years, no candidate for musical fame among our countrymen had appeared who was equally admired by the nation at large. It appears that

[1] 'À peine au sortir de l'enfance', a romance from *Joseph* (1807), with English words by H. M. Milner.

[2] A song from Arne's *Eliza* (1743).

Arne was an Eton boy & intended for the law. But his love for music operated upon him too powerfully even while at Eton either for his own peace or that of his companions, for with a miserable cracked common flute, he used to torment them night and day when not obliged to attend at school.

In 1738 Arne established his reputation as a lyric composer by the admirable manner in which he set Milton's 'Comus'. In this masque or work, he introduced the light, airy, original and pleasing melody wholly different from that of Purcell or Handel, whom hitherto all England had either pillaged or imitated. It was in 1762 that Arne quitted that style of melody to be found in 'Comus' & furnished Vauxhall & the whole kingdom with such songs as improved and polished our national taste. There can be no doubt that his natural & unaffected music will long retain its place in the hearts of every lover of English music. I would particularly call your attention to the exquisite cadence at the end of each verse in the song which I am now going to offer you.

Moonlight Sonata [Op. 27, No. 2]	Beethoven

As a specimen of the great Beethoven I have chosen a work which, although not of large dimensions, represents him in his most poetical & masterly mood.

Beethoven has been a most munificent benefactor to home music, and although able at all times to wield his orchestral fancies with the hands of a giant, has chosen to adopt the pianoforte (thus [a] home instrument) as the agent of some of his largest & most poetic creations: take for instance the entire series of his sonatas, commencing with those ded[icated] to Haydn, Op. 2, and ending with the Op. 111, and you will find a collection of beautiful conceptions, which for sublimity, development, beauty & fancy, have never been surpassed if even equalled by any other composer. Before I present you with this sonata, I cannot forego mentioning to you some of his choice vocal gems, such as the 'Circle of Songs' called in German the 'Lieder Kreis' [*An die ferne Geliebte*, Op. 98], a work which is comparatively unknown but which is available to any private circle.

Schlummerlied [from *Albumblätter*: Op. 124, No. 16]	Schumann

I will play this elegant little piece of Schumann's, so entirely suited to the drawing room. Robert Schumann, my dear personal friend, I cannot allow to be confounded with the musicians of the present romantic school, who are endeavouring to turn day into night. I know Schumann to have been a sincere lover of all that was pure & great in music; his pen has oft shown his appreciation of the great masters. I am inclined to believe that Schumann's present extraordinary reputation is rather due to the superabundant enthusiasm of his disciples than to his own powers; he would have been the last person in the world to have wished himself exalted above Mendelssohn, as has been done by his indiscreet admirers. I have sat <daily> for six or 8 months in years gone by at the Table d'Hôte in Leipzig with Mendelssohn, Schumann & others, and I can witness to the delight with which Schumann husbanded every minute spent in the company of our illustrious friend.

Song, 'The First Violet' [Op. 19, No. 2]	Mendelssohn
Andante and Rondo Capriccioso [Op. 14]	Mendelssohn

Perhaps the music of Mendelssohn has had greater success, both in public & private circles, than any other ever composed; even young ladies who will steadily adhere to the superficial music of the present day still find place in their repertoire for many of the works of this illustrious man. This fact amidst all my grumbling consoles me, & leads me to finish my programme with the hope that by little & little things must present a different aspect, and that the mind & heart which can feel & love Mendelssohn will cease to enjoy the {ephemeral & unintellectual} music which is so abundant and for which I cannot disguise my utter contempt.

Second Sheffield Lecture

19 April 1859
Concert Programme

Pianoforte,
Professor W. S. Bennett, and Mr. Percival Phillips,
with vocal performers

Harpsichord Lessons, P.F.	Handel
Song, 'Rendi il sereno', 'Lord remember David'[1]	Handel
Early Sonata, P.F.	Mozart
Grand Sonata, P.F.	Mozart
Canzonet ['The season comes'?]	Haydn
Sonata, E Flat	Haydn
Duet, P.F. (Symphony [No. 1] in E Flat, [Op. 20])	Spohr
Vocal Duet (Tema e Variazioni)	Rossini
Duet, P.F.	Weber
Solo, P.F. [Caprice in F major, Op. 49]	Hummel
[Selection from] Lieder ohne Worte	Mendelssohn

1 See p. 48.

Bibliography

Archives and Manuscripts

Cambridge. Cambridge University Library, UA CUR 39.10.1. Regulations and notices relating to the professorship of music, 1856–1933.

London. British Library, Additional MSS. 27687–9 and 27693. John Wall Callcott's commonplace book.

———. Royal Musical Society. Concert Committee Minutes and Accounts, 1852–1859.

Longparish, Hants. Bennett's library and papers, in the possession of Barry Sterndale-Bennett. (Includes the lectures in 6 bound volumes.)

Printed Sources and Dissertations

Balchin, Robert, ed. *CPM: The Catalogue of Printed Music in the British Library to 1980*. 62 vols. London, &c.: K. G. Saur, 1981–87.

Banister, Henry C. *George Alexander Macfarren: His Life, Works, and Influence*. London: George Bell and Sons, 1891.

Bashford, Christina. 'John Ella and the Making of the Musical Union.' *Music and British Culture 1785–1914*, ed. Christina Bashford and Leanne Langley (Oxford: Oxford University Press, 2000), 193–214.

———. 'The Late Beethoven Quartets and the London Press, 1836–ca. 1850.' *Musical Quarterly* 84 (2000), 84–122.

———. 'Learning to Listen: Audiences for Chamber Music in Early-Victorian London.' *Journal of Victorian Culture* 4/1 (1999), 25–51.

———. 'Not just "G.": Towards a History of the Programme Note.' *George Grove, Music and Victorian Culture*, ed. Michael Musgrave (London: Palgrave Macmillan, 2003), 115–42.

——— and Leanne Langley, eds. *Music and British Culture, 1785–1914*. Oxford: Oxford University Press, 2000.

Bennett, J. R. Sterndale. *The Life of William Sterndale Bennett*. Cambridge: Cambridge University Press, 1907.

Biddlecombe, George. *English Opera from 1834 to 1864 with Particular Reference to the Works of Michael Balfe*. New York & London: Garland, 1994.

Burney, Charles. *A General History of Music from the Earliest Ages to the Present Period*. 4 vols. London, 1776–89.

———. ——. ed. Frank Mercer. 2 vols. New York: Harcourt, Brace and Co., [1935].

———. *The Present State of Music in Germany, the Netherlands, and United Provinces*. Vol. 1. London: T. Becket and Co., 1773.

The Cambridge University Calendar for the year 1870. Cambridge: Deighton, Bell and Co., [1870].

Chrysander, Friedrich. *G. F. Händel*. 3 vols. Leipzig: Breitkopf & Härtel, 1858–67.

Crotch, William. *Substance of Several Courses of Lectures on Music, read in the University of Oxford, and in the Metropolis*. London: Longman, Rees, Orme, Brown, and Green, 1831. Reprint, ed. Bernarr Rainbow, Calabricken, Ireland: Boethius Press, 1986.

———. *Specimens of Various Styles of Music*. London: R. Birchall, [1807].

Crowest, Frederick J. *Phases of Musical England*. London: Remington & Co., 1881.

Cutler, Janet C. 'The London Institution 1805–1933.' Ph.D. dissertation, Leicester University, 1976.

Dean, Winton. *Handel's Dramatic Oratorios and Masques*. London: Oxford University Press, 1959.

A Descriptive Catalogue of the Lectures Delivered at the London Institution . . . From the Opening of the Theatre . . . 1819 to . . . 1854. London: privately printed, 1854.

Dibble, Jeremy. *Charles Villiers Stanford: Man and Musician*. Oxford: Oxford University Press, 2002.

Duckles, Vincent. 'Musicology.' *The Romantic Age 1800–1914* (The Blackwell History of Music in Britain, 5, ed. Nicholas Temperley, Oxford: Blackwell, 1988), 483–502.

Ehrlich, Cyril. *First Philharmonic: A History of the Royal Philharmonic Society*. Oxford: Clarendon Press, 1995.

———. *The Music Profession in Britain Since the Eighteenth Century*. Oxford: Clarendon Press, 1985.

Fétis, François-Joseph. *The History of Music: How to Understand and Enjoy its Performance*. [A translation of Fétis, *La musique mise à la portée de tout le monde*, Paris, 1830.] London: George Routledge, 1846.

Freemantle, W. T. *Sterndale Bennett and Sheffield*. Sheffield: Pawson & Brailsford, 1919.

Fuhrmann, Christina. 'Continental Opera Englished: *Der Freischütz* in London, 1824.' *Nineteenth-Century Music Review*, 1/1 (2004), 115–42.

Gianturco, Carolyn, and Eleanor McCrickard. *Alessandro Stradella: A Thematic Catalogue of his Compositions*. Stuyvesant, New York: Pendragon Press, 1991.

Gillett, Paula. 'Ambivalent Friendships: Music-Lovers, Amateurs, and Professional Musicians in the Late Nineteenth Century.' *Music and*

British Culture 1785–1914, ed. Christina Bashford and Leanne Langley (Oxford: Oxford University Press, 2000), 321–40.

Goethe, Johann Wolfgang von. *Maximen und Reflexionen, neu geordnet, eingeleitet und erläutert von Günther Müller*. Stuttgart: A. Kröner, [1943].

Hall-Witt, Jennifer L. 'Representing the Audience in the Age of Reform.' *Music and British Culture 1785–1914*, ed. Christina Bashford and Leanne Langley (Oxford: Oxford University Press, 2000), 121–44.

Hawkins, John. *A General History of the Science and Practice of Music*. London, 1776.

Hogarth, George. *Musical History, Biography, and Criticism*. London: John W. Parker, 1835.

Holmes, Edward. *The Life of Mozart, Including his Correspondence*. London: Chapman & Hall, 1845.

Hurd, Michael. 'Opera: 1834–1865'. *The Romantic Age 1800–1914*. The Blackwell History of Music in Britain, 5, ed. Nicholas Temperley (Oxford: Blackwell, 1988), 310–29.

Irving, Howard. *Ancients and Moderns: William Crotch and the Development of Classical Music*. Aldershot: Ashgate, 1999.

Kassler, Jamie Croy. 'The Royal Insitution Music Lectures, 1800–1831: A Preliminary Study', *Royal Musical Association Research Chronicle*, 19 (1983–85), 1–30.

———. *The Science of Music in Britain, 1714–1830: A Catalogue of Writings, Lectures and Inventions*. 2 vol. New York & London: Garland, 1979.

Kiesewetter, Rafael Georg. *History of the Modern Music of Western Europe*. [A translation by Robert Müller of Kiesewetter's *Geschichte der europäisch-abendländischen oder unser heutigen Musik*, Leipzig, 1834.] London: T. C. Newby, 1848.

Krummel, Donald W. 'Music Publishing'. *Music in Britain: The Romantic Age 1800–1914*, ed. N. Temperley (Oxford: Blackwell, 1988), 46–59.

Loewenberg, Alfred. *Annals of Opera 1597–1940*. 3rd ed. Totowa, New Jersey: Rowman & Littlefield, 1978.

Mackerness, E. D. *Somewhere Further North: A History of Music in Sheffield*. Sheffield: J. W. Northend Ltd, 1974.

Marx, Adolph Bernhard. *The Music of the Nineteenth Century and its Culture*. Translated by A. H. Wehrhan and C. N. Macfarren. London: Robert Cocks and Co., 1854. [This was published in advance of the German original, *Die Musik des neunzehnten Jahrhunderts und ihre Pflege: Methode der Musik* (Leipzig, 1855).]

Massenkeil, Günther, ed. *Cantatas by Giacomo Carissimi*. The Italian Cantata in the Seventeenth Century, 2. New York and London: Garland, 1986.

Morley, Thomas. *A Plain and Easy Introduction to Practical Music*, ed. Alec Harman. London: J. M. Dent & Sons, 1952.

Musgrave, Michael. *The Musical Life of the Crystal Palace*. Cambridge: Cambridge University Press, 1995.

O'Leary, Arthur. 'Sir William Sterndale Bennett: A Brief Review of his Life and Works.' *Proceedings of the Musical Association* 8 (1881–82), 123–41.

Olleson, Philip. *Samuel Wesley: The Man and his Music*. Woodbridge, Suffolk: The Boydell Press, 2003.

Peter, Philip H. and Julian Rushton. 'Potter, (Philip) Cipriani (Hambly)'. *The New Grove Dictionary of Music and Musicians*, ed. Stanley Sadie, revised edition (London: Macmillan, 2001), 20, 221–3.

Playford, John, ed. *Catch that Catch Can, or The Musical Companion . . . To which is now added a Second Book containing Dialogues, Glees, Ayres, and Ballads, &c. Some for Two, Three, Foure Voyces*. London: J. Playford, 1667.

Porter, William Smith. *Sheffield Literary and Philosophical Society: A Centenary Retrospect 1822–1922*. Sheffield: 1922.

Reid, Charles. *The Music Monster: A Biography of James William Davison*. London: Quartet Books, 1984.

Rennert, Jonathan. *William Crotch 1755–1847: Composer, Artist, Teacher*. Lavenham, Suffolk: Terence Dalton Limited, 1975.

Reynolds, Joshua. *Discourses Delivered to Students of the Royal Academy*. London: James Carpenter, 1842.

Rimbault, Edward F. 'Memoir of William Byrd.' In William Byrd, *A Mass for Five Voices*, ed. Rimbault, London: Musical Antiquarian Society, 1841.

Rushton, Julian. 'Gluck, Christopher Willibald Ritter von: 6. Paris, 1774–9'. *The New Grove Dictionary of Music and Musicians*, ed. Stanley Sadie, revised edition (London: Macmillan, 2001), 10, 39–41.

[Sainsbury, John.] *Dictionary of Musicians, from the Earliest Ages to the Present Time*. 2 vols. London: Sainsbury & Co., 1825.

Schindler, Anton Felix, *The Life of Beethoven*, ed. Ignaz Moscheles. London: Henry Colburn, 1841.

Schoelcher, Victor. *The Life of Handel*. Translated from the French by James Lowe. London: Trübner and Co., 1857.

Scholes, Percy A. *The Mirror of Music 1844–1944*. London: Novello, Oxford University Press, 1947.

Scott, Derek B. 'Blackface Minstrels, Black Minstrels, and their Reception in England.' *Europe, Empire, and Spectacle in Nineteenth-Century British Music*, ed. Rachel Cowgill and Julian Rushton (Aldershot: Ashgate, 2006), 265–80.

Silantien, John J. 'The Part-Song in England, 1837–1914.' DMA thesis, University of Illinois, 1980.

Simpson, Harold. *A Century of Ballads 1810–1910*. London: Mills & Boon Ltd, 1910.

Smith, William C. *Concerning Handel: His Life and Works*. London: Cassell and Company Ltd, 1948.

Spark, Frederick R., and Joseph Bennett. *History of the Leeds Musical Festivals 1858–1889*. Leeds: Fred. R. Spark & Son, Richard Jackson, and London: Novello, Ewer & Co., 1892.

Spark, William. *Musical Memories*. London: Swan, Sonnenschein & Co., 1888.

Stanford, Charles Villiers. 'William Sterndale Bennett.' *Musical Quarterly* 2 (1916), 628–57.

Taylor, Edward. *Gresham College: Three Inaugural Lectures, delivered in the Theatre of the City of London School, January 29th, 31st, and February 1st, 1838*. London: Richard and John Edward Taylor, 1838.

Temperley, Nicholas. 'Bennett, William Sterndale.' *The New Grove Dictionary of Music and Musicians*, ed. Stanley Sadie, revised edition (London: Macmillan, 2001), 3, 281–4.

———. 'The English Romantic Opera'. *Victorian Studies* 9 (1966), 293–301.

———. 'Instrumental Music in England, 1800–1850.' Ph.D. dissertation, Cambridge University, 1959.

———. 'Mozart's Influence on English Music.' *Music & Letters* 42 (1961), 307–18.

———. 'Musical Nationalism in English Romantic Opera.' *The Lost Chord: Essay on Victorian Music*, ed. N. Temperley (Bloomington, Indiana: Indiana University Press, 1989), 143–57.

———. 'Schumann and Sterndale Bennett.' *19th Century Music* 12 (1989), 207–20.

———. 'Sterndale Bennett and the Lied.' *Musical Times* 116 (1975), 958–61, 1060–63.

———. 'Xenophilia in British Musical History.' *Nineteenth-Century British Music Studies 1*, ed. Bennett Zon (Aldershot: Ashgate, 1999), 3–19.

———, ed. *The London Pianoforte School 1766–1860*. 20 vols. New York & London: Garland, 1982–85.

Turle, James. 'Introduction' to John Wilbye, *The First Set of Madrigals to 3, 4, 5 and 6 Voices*, ed. Turle. London: Chappell, for the Musical Antiquarian Society, [1846].

Walker, Ernest. *A History of Music in England*. Oxford: Oxford University Press, 1907.

Warrack, John. *Carl Maria von Weber*. 2nd ed. Cambridge: Cambridge University Press, 1976.

———. *Weber in London 1826: Selections from Weber's Letters to His Wife*. London: Oswald Wolff Limited, 1976.

Wilbye, John. *The First Set of English Madrigals to 3, 4, 5, and 6 Voices*, ed.

James Turle. London: Chappell, for the Musical Antiquarian Society, [1846].

Williams, Charles Francis Abdy. *A Short Historical Account of Degrees in Music at Oxford and Cambridge*. London, 1893.

Williamson, Rosemary. *William Sterndale Bennett: A Descriptive Thematic Catalogue*. Oxford: Clarendon Press, 1996.

Winstanley, D. A. *Unreformed Cambridge*. Cambridge: Cambridge University Press, 1935.

Wollenberg, Susan. *Music at Oxford in the Eighteenth and Nineteenth Centuries*. Oxford: Oxford University Press, 2001.

Yang, Yunchung. 'William Sterndale Bennett's Fantasia in its Historical Context.' DMA dissertation, University of Illinois at Urbana-Champaign, 2001.

Zaslaw, Neil. *Mozart's Symphonies: Context, Performance Practice, Reception*. Oxford: Oxford University Press, 1989.

Index

Personal characterizations assume 'English' unless another nationality is stated.
n. = footnote